SALESFORCE:
BUILDING THE ROI BUSINESS CASE

SALESFORCE: BUILDING THE ROI BUSINESS CASE

Daniel Elman · Nucleus Research

Copyright © 2019, Nucleus Research. All rights reserved.

Printed in the United States of America. No part of this publication may be reproduced, stored in, or introduced into a retrieval system, or transmitted, in any form, or by any means (electronic, mechanical, photocopying, recording, or otherwise) without the prior written permission of the copyright owner and the publisher of this book.

Published by Nucleus Research
ISBN 9781088939918
First printing: August, 2019

All brand names and product names used in this book are trademarks, registered trademarks, or trade names of their respective holders. All statements contained herein are the opinion of the author and should not be considered professional advice.

TABLE OF CONTENTS

Foreword vii
Introduction 1
Salesforce Products 5
Common Benefits of Salesforce Technology 19
What Are These Metrics? 25
Case Studies 31
    Financial Institution 33
    Sequoia Financial Group 41
    Matouk 47
    ICS+ 55
    Financial Services 61
    VVMWare Inc. 67
    Superior Pool Spa and Leisure 75
    Food Producer 83
    BCBS Michigan 91
    Paducah Bank 97
    Insurance Company 103
    Aspect 109
    Trilogy Financial 115
    Shazam 123
    Rack Room Shoes 129
    Rosetta Stone 135
    Life Time Fitness 143
    Stanley Healthcare 149
    Amplify 155
    5P Consulting 161
Conclusion 169

FOREWORD

Salesforce has been a pioneer in the software-as-a-service space since its founding in 1999 when Marc Benioff saw how cloud technology reduced IT cost and complexity and allowed businesses to fully leverage the power of the internet. In fact, Salesforce was among the drivers of the early-2000s mass exodus to the cloud—anyone remember the "No Software" mascot?—by being first to demonstrate how cloud tech could address major shortcomings of the on-premises deployments, like unwieldy upgrades and the difficulties of connecting disparate systems from far apart. Fast forward to today and Salesforce is among the leading cloud vendors, pulling in over $10 billion in revenue last year alone. It has maintained its position over the years through continuous technological innovation, savvy market education and awareness campaigns, strategic partnerships and acquisitions, and a steadfast commitment to delivering real-world value to its customers.

Perhaps the most telling indicator of Salesforce's dominance in the market is the myriad of positive customers testimonials and outcomes. Their customers don't need to use arcane financial metrics or vague platitudes to characterize their results from Salesforce because it delivers legitimate ROI. The technology helps customers to simplify their businesses, reduce complexity and cost, and increase total profits, outcomes that can easily be captured with traditional ROI calculations.

Recently, Salesforce has increasingly turned to acquisition to accelerate growth with major acquisitions of MuleSoft, the integration platform, and Tableau, the data visualization and business intelligence tool, announced in the last year. These moves underscore the fact that Salesforce has developed into a mature company and organic growth alone can no longer satisfy growth demands.

One thing that hasn't changed as the organization has grown from a startup to an enterprise behemoth is Salesforce's commitment to social responsibility. It is committed to philanthropy and enacting positive social change through the 1-1-1 model where one percent of time, technology, and resources are pledged to philanthropic causes. Even the act of bringing a product like the Philanthropy Cloud to market shows how Salesforce has the expertise, technology, and legitimate interest in fostering social good that set it apart from the "robber baron corporations" dominating the headlines. Salesforce stands out for the right reasons by prioritizing value over short-term profits and societal good over personal gain; with this model it will continue to excel for a long time.

—Ian Campbell, *CEO Nucleus Research*

INTRODUCTION

Salesforce, formerly salesforce.com, played a leading role in bringing cloud computing to the mainstream. It was the first major vendor to demonstrate how the software-as-a-service model can benefit customers with reduced cost and time spent implementing upgrades and dramatically increased product accessibility from being hosted on the Internet instead of in on-site servers. It entered the market in 1999 with its cloud-based CRM solution and has grown to offer a portfolio of enterprise applications across sales, service, marketing, analytics, commerce, and infrastructure.

The purpose of this guide is to help prospective technology buyers understand the solutions Salesforce offers and formulate a compelling business case in favor of Salesforce to financial decision makers. This guide lays out the products that Salesforce currently offers with the most commonly realized business benefits according to Nucleus findings from ROI case study data. It also includes recent ROI case studies involving Salesforce customers and technology. The final section defines the common financial metrics and types of benefits used when making enterprise purchasing decisions and explains to the reader how to present a compelling, data-backed business case to leadership.

This Salesforce guide contains business case studies representing the collective work of Nucleus Research, with analysis of Salesforce deployments over the past two years. This guide is designed to serve as a tool for evaluating a potential Salesforce deployment on *value*, not marketing, by showing buyers how Salesforce has delivered financial returns to organizations just like yours. This research is conducted independently of Salesforce, and represents the real achieved results of organizations' deployments. Although every deployment is unique, the case studies show how organizations across size, industry, and maturity can achieve results. While not every story will align to your business, we hope that you are able to see yourself in some of these stories and use others' experiences to help drive your own journey.

For each case study, Nucleus Research analyzed the costs of software, hardware, personnel, consulting, and training over a three-year period to quantify the customer's investment in Salesforce technology. Direct and indirect benefits were also quantified over the three-year period. All time savings were then multiplied by a correction factor to account for the inefficient transfer of time between time saved and additional time worked.

Nucleus Research has conducted more than seven hundred ROI case studies in its 20-year history. It is the only independent technology research firm that is certified by the National Association of State Boards of Accountancy (NASBA). This means our calculations are done the same way your CFO does them: no tricks, no magic.

SALESFORCE PRODUCTS

Customer 360

Over the past twenty years, Salesforce has had a vision to help organizations gain a single view of their customers. With this view, organizations can know their customers and truly offer them a continuous, personalized experience across all company touchpoints.

Salesforce Customer 360 is the realization of that vision, and will help companies predict customer behavior, personalize their experience, and deliver the right service at the right time. It is the key to driving success across your organization, and for connecting to your customers in a whole new way.

APPLICATIONS

Salesforce Customer 360 includes applications for every touchpoint in a customer's journey. Let's take a moment to review each of the solutions:

- **Sales** provides sales teams the power to close deals, increase productivity, fill pipelines with solid leads, and score more wins without software, hardware, or speed limits.
- **Service** allows you to enhance your customer support—from call-center software to self-service portals. Get more responsive, intuitive, and flexible service solutions that help you anticipate your customers' needs.
- **Marketing & Journeys** allows you to build and deliver 1-to-1 (or

personalized) customer journeys powered by the intelligent marketing platform for email, mobile, social, digital advertising, and DMP.
- **Commerce** enables you to build better customer experiences and vastly improve (or increase) conversion rates.
- **Engagement Apps:** allow you to build custom apps connected to Salesforce and get your apps to market faster with Heroku cloud services and developer experience.
- **Platform & Ecosystem:** Customer 360 Platform allows you to streamline, automate, and mobilize any business process using the secure, scalable Customer 360 Platform. In addition, you can build, run, and manage apps.
- **MuleSoft Anypoint Platform** (Integration & APIs) offers integration. Connect any app, data, or device, whether in the cloud or on-premises, in one place; and bring data from any system, like SAP, Oracle, Workday, and more, directly into Salesforce.
- **Einstein Analytics** enables you to make more intelligent, data-driven decisions that guide your business forward. Artificial intelligence has simplified the entire analytics workflow, taking you from data to insight to action in minutes.
- **Industries** helps you find tailored solutions designed to meet the specific needs of your industry (including Financial Services, Healthcare, and Philanthropy), and to transform every aspect of your business with Salesforce.
- **Community** provides the use of templates to quickly launch pre-built, use-case-specific solutions for your customers and partners. Or, you can start with partner-built industry-specific solutions and components.
- **Trailhead** (Learning & Reskilling) is a free online learning platform that empowers everyone to learn the skills needed for the Fourth Industrial Revolution; and with myTrailhead, customers can personalize Trailhead for their business, with their brand and content, to reinvent corporate learning and enablement.
- **Quip** (Productivity) for Salesforce brings productivity apps directly into the #1 CRM. Close deals, plan campaigns, and respond to customers faster by enhancing your Salesforce experience with templated documents and workflows. Bring structured and unstructured data together in one modern, integrated experience.

PLATFORM

The Customer 360 Platform is an underlying set of services like AI, Mobile, Voice, etc. available to Salesforce apps and your custom apps. As Salesforce continues to add new platform services like Blockchain, your apps automatically get better and better. Let's dive into each of these services so we can better understand the benefits.

- **Mobile:** All your Salesforce data is available on your mobile device. You can also build engaging mobile apps, with clicks or code.
- **AI:** Einstein is a layer of intelligence, spanning the entire Customer 360 Platform, that allows you to discover insights, predict outcomes, recommend actions, and automate workflows. Einstein includes out-of-the-box AI features for Sales, Service, Marketing, and Commerce, as well as programmatic and declarative AI services for admins and developers (like voice, vision, and language). Now, irrespective of their skillset, everyone can benefit from AI—embedded where you work.
- **Vision:** With Einstein Vision, every developer and admin can harness the power of image recognition in their apps by training deep learning models to recognize their brand, products, and more. You can classify images at scale, detect objects within images, and even extract text from documents.
- **Voice:** This provides the ability to talk to Salesforce on any device. With speech recognition and natural language processing, Einstein Voice allows you to log meeting notes conversationally, get a daily briefing on the smart speaker of your choice, and drive analytics dashboards with your voice. You can even create Einstein Voice Bots and expose them on smart speakers so your customers can get support on their favorite device.
- **Security:** The trust services of the Salesforce Platform are available to every customer out of the box. With Salesforce Shield, customers who need additional controls and protection can leverage an additional suite of built-in services to help with priorities such as compliance, driven by industry regulations and internal policies as well as insight and control.
- **Builder:** Salesforce gives you the tools you need to build apps quickly and declaratively with the Lightning Platform. Whether you're building mobile apps, customizing pages, or building communities for customers and partners, Salesforce's low-code and no-code builders let

- **IoT:** Harness IoT data to build, iterate and deploy proactive sales, service or marketing business processes. With their APIs, you can connect any product or device to Salesforce. With Field Service Lightning, you can take a service action in Salesforce.
- **Blockchain:** Share valuable data in a secure, tamperproof, and transparent way, creating visibility between your partners.

you drag and drop components and visually automate workflows to deliver modern user experiences on any device.

Sales

- Sales Cloud
- Configure, Price, Quote
- Sales Cloud Einstein

Salesforce offers end-to-end functionality across the full sales cycle. **Sales Cloud** offers functionality for contact management, lead generation and capture, identifying opportunities, contracting, and quoting. It is also built to enable automation of repeated user tasks like data capture and includes built-in analytical capabilities for reporting and tracking KPIs.

Configure, Price, Quote is a sales tool that allows for quick quote generation—in minutes. Before auto-quoting tools, sales reps had to build quotes manually out of spreadsheets, which could take days or weeks. The quoting process is automated according to rules established in the company pricing model to ensure complete accuracy.

Sales Cloud Einstein leverages artificial intelligence (AI) to automate predictive analysis of CRM data within Sales Cloud. It automates data entry with Einstein Activity Capture and is continuously retrained on the new data as it enters the system to better "learn" how to drive successful sales. Lead and Opportunity Scoring analyzes data and predicts which leads and opportunities are most likely to close. Einstein Opportunity and Account Insights analyze account engagement and relevant external news to keep reps up to date with account activity. Sales Analytics and Einstein Forecasting help uncover insights, surface trends in data, and predict future sales.

Service

- Service Cloud

- Field Service Lightning

Service Cloud is built on Salesforce Customer 360, giving organizations a 360-degree view of their customers with the goal of delivering smarter, faster, and more personalized service. It includes case management, agent desktop, integration with legacy data systems, pre-built integration apps, support ticketing, knowledge base, routing and escalation, and queue management. It allows for the automation of service processes such as auto-assignment and escalation of cases. It can streamline workflows and surface key articles, topics, and experts to transform the agent experience. Companies can engage customers across a vast array of channels including messaging, video, self-service communities, web chat, in-app, email, phone, in-person, and even IoT-connected products.

Field Service Lightning is built on the Service Cloud platform and allows companies to schedule employees intelligently (based on skill level and/or physical location), assign work, and gain complete visibility into sales and service operations from the contact center to the field. Contact center agents, dispatchers, managers, and mobile employees (be they service technicians or field sales representatives) all work off a complete view of the customer with full context into cases. The Field Service Lightning mobile app allows mobile employees and contractors to share job updates, access knowledge articles, view and update vehicle stock or inventory, collect signatures, and generate service reports from any mobile device, regardless of connectivity. The Einstein Vision capability uses image recognition to immediately identify assets and parts in images to ensure the correct product part is fixed or replaced, which eliminates confusion and additional trips to and from the site. Companies can also delineate service territories, track the location and status of active cases, create templates to standardize repeated tasks, and generate service reports.

Marketing

- Marketing Cloud
- Pardot

Salesforce Marketing Cloud helps marketers manage relationships and create campaigns. Content creation and management tools allow marketers to create custom media for campaigns and track the deployment and results of these campaigns. Predictive analytics on the platform help identify which channel or type of outreach would be most effective with a particular customer. Journey Builder helps marketing teams to create campaigns based on the customer behavior, needs, and demographics. The platform leverages event-driven triggers to automatically take pre-determined actions based on customer actions.

Salesforce Pardot is a complete B2B marketing automation solution, delivering cutting-edge lead management, faster sales cycles, and a smarter, more personalized customer experience. Through intelligent features including recently announced Einstein Campaign Insights and Einstein Behavior, Pardot empowers marketers to establish more leads and arms sales teams with personalized content at the right time. Pardot can manage and execute e-mail marketing campaigns and track the effectiveness and ROI of campaigns to identify successful practices and eliminate those that are unsuccessful.

Commerce

- Commerce Cloud
- B2C Commerce
- B2B Commerce

Commerce Cloud, formerly Demandware, is the leading enterprise cloud commerce platform that empowers companies to build, manage, and deploy custom e-commerce experiences to customers on multiple channels and devices. Brands grow on Commerce Cloud because they have access to a complete Salesforce Customer 360 built for the entire customer journey—meaning they can launch quickly and innovate easily, realizing faster time to value. They also have Einstein, which makes AI accessible for intelligent data-driven decisions and personalized shopping experiences.

B2C Commerce allows for storefront creation and provides resources and processing for e-commerce sites. It includes tools to reduce abandoned carts, merges with social media to gather more complete customer information, and is optimized with mobile-first capabilities like one-touch payment and responsive design. Companies can manage marketing and merchandising campaigns with the system, and Einstein AI enables personalized recommendations and helps increase revenue with insights around customer purchasing behavior.

B2B Commerce enables users to quickly build self-service online storefronts that connect with retailers and distributors to purchase goods from their brand. It is designed with business-to-business features like custom catalogs, complex product configurations, contracting, and reorders. It also includes AI capabilities for smart recommendations, automated data gathering and analysis.

Engagement

- Heroku

The **Heroku** cloud platform allows companies to build, deploy, monitor, and scale applications while mitigating the complication that comes with managing the hardware and servers (on-premise or cloud). Heroku integrates natively with Salesforce data which allows organizations to leverage the combined capabilities of the Lightning and Heroku platforms and create custom applications that sync data directly to workflows in Salesforce.

Platform and Ecosystem

- Lightning
- Heroku Enterprise

Salesforce Lightning is a component-based application development framework that simplifies application creation and configuration with graphical, click-based interaction that is simple even for users without programming experience. Lightning App Builder allows users to create custom apps in a drag-and-drop environment, and the newly open-sourced Lightning Web Components allow users to build these applications on Salesforce and other platforms.

Heroku Enterprise includes the Heroku development platform with governance and management capabilities that large organizations require. It includes the standard Heroku development capabilities along with stronger access controls; Private Spaces which deliver network-level isolation for workloads with strict security requirements; and Shield Private Spaces which include additional compliance features. Heroku Enterprise combines the flexibility of an open development platform with the security that a large enterprise needs.

Integration

- MuleSoft

MuleSoft helps organizations change and innovate faster by making it easy to connect to the world's applications, data, and devices. MuleSoft AnyPoint Platform is the only platform to connect to APIs and integrations in one product—whether the data is in Salesforce or not, or if it's on-premises or in the cloud—to build an application network of pluggable and reusable services. By unlocking data across the enterprise with application networks, organizations can easily deliver new revenue channels, increase operational efficiency, and create differentiated customer experiences.

Analytics

- Einstein Analytics

Einstein Analytics, formerly Wave Analytics, is an augmented analytics platform for managing and analyzing data, discovering new insights, creating custom AI models, and building dashboards, reports, and visualizations to make data actionable and drive business decisions. Einstein Discovery automatically analyzes data and surfaces predictive insights and recommendations, in context. Einstein Analytics is accessible on any device, and advances like Einstein Voice and natural language search allow users to interact with data conversationally by asking questions of their reports and dashboards. Pre-built templates, KPIs, and reports for various departments and industries save time and increase usability out of the box.

Industries

- Financial Services Cloud
- Health Cloud
- Government Cloud
- Philanthropy Cloud
- Education Cloud
- Nonprofit Cloud

Financial Services Cloud is an industry solution built specifically for firms across wealth management, banking, and insurance. It provides a 360-degree view of clients, customers, and policyholders, enabling firms to deliver personalized, proactive service. It includes productivity tools to gather and surface relevant data and templates for workflows specific to financial services, which reduces the amount of customer configuration needed. It also leverages Einstein AI to show trends, perform analyses, and recommend actions.

Health Cloud is an industry solution built specifically for healthcare and life sciences. It is a cloud-based patient relationship management platform that helps build stronger relationships and deliver more personalized care and experiences across channels, with a 360-degree view of the patient, member, or customer. Health Cloud unifies patient data through the integration of EHR data, treatment plans, patient preferences, social determinants of health, and more. It is a hub for healthcare team collaboration across a patient's caregiver network. It simplifies IT for healthcare and offers a secure, cloud-based environment for creating stronger relationships with patients and delivering more timely, personalized care.

Government Cloud is an industry solution that is a portion of Salesforce's multitenant, public cloud infrastructure—specifically partitioned for use by Federal, state, and local government agencies, as well as government contractors. It supports compliance standards including FedRAMP Moderate, DoD IL4, SOC, ISO 27001/27018, and PCI. It allows users to securely develop and deploy applications and associated data.

Philanthropy Cloud is an industry solution that empowers corporations to put their values into action by connecting employees to causes in an easy-to-use and centralized way through giving, matching, and volunteering tools. Companies can track and manage their philanthropic goals as well as bring employees and communities together to improve the state of the world. Philanthropy Cloud helps companies attract and retain talent, elevate their brand, and contribute positively to their communities and the world.

Education Cloud is an industry solution that connects students, staff, and alumni with integrated solutions for K-12 and higher education, providing 360-degree views to engage all constituents through connected experiences. Its foundation is Education Data Architecture (EDA), which provides a flexible data architecture to configure Salesforce out of the box for education. Purpose-built applications include Salesforce Advisor Link for student success and Gift Entry Manager (GEM) for pledge and gift management.

Nonprofit Cloud is an industry solution that connects an entire organization across all the core functions of a nonprofit: marketing, fundraising, and program management. It offers a complete platform to gain a 360-degree view of constituent engagement, revenue, and measures of social impact.

Communities

- Community Cloud
- Community Builder

Community Cloud is a social platform that enables communication and engagement among a company's employees, customers, and partners. It leverages Chatter for chat to fuel collaboration. It can be integrated with CRM and e-commerce systems to allow organizations to communicate directly with customers and allow customers to make purchases directly within Community Cloud. Internally, it can be used for information sharing, human resources functions, and to enable geographically disparate teams to work together efficiently.

Community Builder includes templates for self-service creation of custom digital communities. It allows users to style the community with custom branding, modify pages and components to customize content and layout, and deliver the community on any device.

Enablement

- myTrailhead

myTrailhead is the Salesforce online learning experience platform that allows organizations to support employee up-skilling and enablement with custom branding and organization-specific content. Trail Maker is a guided setup tool for employers to create their own custom content for employees. Trailhead Profiles for each employee show skills, expertise, and progress in the myTrailhead system. Trail Mixer allows employees to create and share custom learning paths from the available materials within myTrailhead. Trail Tracker allows managers to track and assign progress and includes gamified leaderboards to spur adoption.

Productivity

- Quip

Salesforce Quip is a collaboration and productivity tool that includes chat, word processing, spreadsheets, presentation software, and content co-creation. Teams can collaborate within the solution in real time to reduce meetings and manage version control. Quip LiveApps connects users directly to live CRM data so that collaborators are always looking at the most up-to-date information. Quip is now embedded within Sales Cloud, Service Cloud, and PRM, allowing teams to incorporate collaborative documents, spreadsheets, slides, and chatrooms within Salesforce objects and records.

Customer Success

- Success Cloud

Salesforce's 150,000 customers utilize **Success Cloud** to achieve business value faster. With Success Cloud, every customer has access to resources, experts, and services infused with 20+ years of best practices and insight from Salesforce experts along every step of their journey. Offerings available through Success Cloud include learning resources to get answers fast, learning on-demand, connecting with peers through online communities, and help and training support. Users also have access to Salesforce experts (such as success managers and specialists) who provide 1:1 coaching, guidance, and 24/7 phone support through customer success and support plans; and access to Salesforce certified architects and consultants.

Essentials

- Salesforce Essentials

Salesforce Essentials makes it possible for small businesses to leverage the power of Salesforce to build stronger customer relationships with combined sales and support CRM that is easy to use, set up, and maintain—for just $25/user/month. The feature-rich platform is simplified to include the basic functionality for sales and service that is easy and inexpensive to set up, use, and maintain. It includes a mobile app and Einstein intelligence to help small business sales teams save time and sell more intelligently.

Trailhead—Salesforce's interactive, online learning environment—is free and seamlessly integrated with Salesforce Essentials, and will guide customers through a fun and easy setup. Salesforce Essentials' infusion with Einstein empowers small businesses to keep customer records up to date automatically without tedious manual data entry. It includes powerful customer support productivity tools, which help automate repetitive service tasks so that companies can deliver service faster and build a self-service support site to help customers find answers to their questions.

Since Salesforce Essentials is built on the Salesforce platform, small businesses don't need to worry about outgrowing their CRM—they can upgrade their system quickly and easily to meet growing demand. In addition, customers can use AppExchange to access an ecosystem of business apps that integrate seamlessly with Salesforce, extending the platform to every department and every industry.

COMMON BENEFITS OF SALESFORCE TECHNOLOGY

Salesforce customers span organizations of all sizes in every industry, and Salesforce works with its customers and partners to meet the specific requirements of its customers' businesses. This effort starts with the Salesforce sales team and product experts who help customers identify areas of their organizations that can be improved or transformed with technology. The effort extends to the partners and consultants who help implement and customize the software to the unique requirements of the customer business and it continues throughout the customer deployment lifespan, with proactive support for troubleshooting, sharing best practices, and ultimately maximizing the value that Salesforce delivers.

Although the organizations are diverse with many unique use cases, we have found in our research at Nucleus that there are many common benefits which organizations tend to receive from Salesforce technology. At its core, any valuable business software makes users more efficient and successful in their roles. Salesforce technology accomplishes this in a number of ways such as by reducing repeated manual tasks like data entry and prospect research, delivering insights and information to users in-context that make them more effective in their roles, making data accessible to everyone, and empowering non-data scientists to perform valuable analysis with a common data model and self-service tools.

Increased User Productivity and Organizational Efficiency

Salesforce solutions are built to help the end user make the most out of thei time. For example, Salesforce data is centralized to minimize time spent searching for information across different departments and directories: it can surface insights about potential customers prior to a meeting to reduce time spent searching the Web for conversation points. Einstein, the AI component, can recommend next actions that statistically maximize the chance of winning deals and identify the opportunities most likely to close, allowing sales teams to maximize the return on their efforts. End user productivity typically increases by approximately five to fifteen percent, with some customers reporting increases of over twenty percent.

Along with increasing productivity on an individual user level, the technology allows entire departments to streamline operations and run more efficiently. This translates to fewer errors and the ability to redeploy staff to other value-add activities, or to reducing headcount without disrupting operations. Customers can often handle significant growth without needing new hires from the efficiency improvements afforded by Salesforce. One customer's organization doubled revenue in three years, and managed the increased complexity and workload without increasing headcount. On average, customers were able to redeploy or avoid the hire of one to four full time equivalent (FTE) staff.

Simplified IT Environment and Reduced IT Cost

Salesforce pioneered the software-as-a-service (SaaS) delivery model and is a leading provider of cloud technology to this day. For organizations transitioning from an on-premises deployment, moving to the cloud allows them to jettison the labor costs and hardware associated with managing the software. It allows updates to be pushed to customers automatically and installed without taking the system out of service, thereby minimizing disruption to the business and the demand on IT staff. Nucleus found that cloud deployments have an average 2.26 times lower total cost of ownership (TCO) than on-premises deployments with an average payback period that is nine months shorter.

Custom report and application designs with low-code environments and drag-and-drop tools allow line-of-business users to create custom apps on the fly without IT involvement. Additionally, Salesforce has an extensive online user community and knowledge base where users can post questions and share best practices, reducing the need for IT troubleshooting. Out-of-the-box templates and industry-specific functionality reduce the need for customization of the software and lead to shorter implementation cycles.

Improved Data Management and Increased Use of Analytics

Part of Salesforce's mission is to enable data transparency to help customers create a data-driven culture of trust and accountability. Salesforce's SaaS delivery model allows data to be centralized and visible to all users (with proper authentication and permission), breaking down silos and affording leadership a 360-degree view of the company. With data centralized and formatted according to a common data model, customers can perform analytics without needing extensive data science resources to build models and interpret results. This makes data accessible throughout the organization and allows leadership to become more data-driven, relying less on intuition or "gut feeling" to make decisions. Many customers report being able to track metrics and create forecasts that were not possible before Salesforce due to disparate data or lack of technical expertise.

While it is somewhat abstract to quantify the exact value that improved data quality and management practices can deliver, we have identified time savings from less time spent searching for data and formatting it for analysis. Typically, organizations can reduce the time spent tracking down and preparing data for analysis by five to 20 percent. It is estimated that 80 percent of the analytics life cycle is spent centralizing, cleansing, and formatting data for analysis, so any time savings in this block allows companies to dedicate more time to the value-add part of the cycle: analyzing data and deriving insights from it.

Increased Profits

A software project's success should ultimately be reflected in the company's bottom line. When workers are enabled to be more efficient, informed, and accurate, they produce more high-quality work products that drive profits. Lead scoring and next-best-action recommendations equip sales representatives to win deals at higher rate, self-service applications and analytics allow for fast and reliable data-backed decision making, and automated marketing outreach and prospect identification can increase lead generation.

The exact profit increases are variable and depend on the organization size and industry, the Salesforce technology implemented, and maturity of the deployment, among other factors.

Increased Total ROI from Unifying Data, Departments, and Processes on a Single Platform

Since all of the different modules and products offered are built on the same backend cloud infrastructure, cross-functional applications, workflows, and analyses can leverage connected information from disparate departments to enable increased visibility and more comprehensive data-backed insights. Having information centralized on the Salesforce platform allows organizations to eliminate duplicated date entry and information requests across silos to increase the efficiency of end users. By not having to pay for separate data storage, maintenance, and preparation, organizations can consolidate those associated costs. By increasing the quality and depth of insights, optimizing user productivity, and reducing repeated labor, and reducing IT and data storage costs, organizations can realize increased total ROI.

WHAT ARE THESE METRICS?

One of the really great things about finance is that there's nothing new. Financial metrics have been around since the beginning of time and haven't changed since. Early cavemen performed rudimentary return on investment (ROI) assessments when they decided to go hunting for food. This is where the idea of a cost-benefit analysis started: "How cold is it outside this cave versus how hungry am I and how long do I need to hunt to gather enough food?" Who knew finance was actually the oldest profession?

Unfortunately, from the simple assessments made during the Stone Age, today we get complex words and three-letter acronyms that make finance appear more difficult. But in fact, nothing has really changed. There are two questions we still ask: is it worth it, and how long until I cover my investment? We answer that with ROI and Payback Period and that's why those are the two most valuable metrics to use when building a business case, and really the only two you need to know.

Of course, if finance were just two metrics then finance classes would last an hour, and there'd be a lot of unemployed finance professors and consultants. To avoid this potential unemployment crisis, a bunch of less useful metrics were created including NPV, TCO, and IRR to keep students studying and consultants billing. Let's demystify these metrics and understand what they are telling us, and, more importantly, what they aren't telling us.

Return on Investment (ROI) is a metric you already understand. It's the annual return you receive on an investment and it's the same percentage number a bank tells you when you deposit funds. If the bank is offering you a 5% interest rate then you know if you deposit $100 today, a year from now the bank will give you $5 and you'll still have your $100 deposit.

Calculating the ROI of an investment is easy if you know the return. It's the total return you expect (in this case, $5) divided by your investment (here it's $100). So, in this example, 5 divided by 100 = 0.05 or 5%. That's all there is to it. The greater the annual benefit, the higher the ROI; while the higher the initial investment, the lower the ROI.

At Nucleus we use a three-year time horizon for assessing the ROI of a project. Our analysts add the net benefits (total benefits less total costs in the year) for each of the three years then divide by 3 for an average annual net benefit number. That smooths any impact of initial year rollout or deployment costs and provides a more realistic assessment of the projects' ongoing ROI.

So, the calculation for ROI is nothing more than:

$$ROI = \frac{((\text{NET BENEFIT IN Y1} + \text{NET BENEFIT IN Y2} + \text{NET BENEFIT IN Y3}) / 3)}{\text{TOTAL INITIAL COST}}$$

Now you might find people who try to make the ROI calculation more complex by using phrases such a "risk-weighted ROI" or "three-year ROI" instead of "annual ROI." These are false calculations used to mislead the buyer rather than provide an accurate assessment. If you're not sure, think about the bank. If your bank doesn't use the metric, you shouldn't either.

Payback Period is nothing more than time needed before you cover your investment. Let's go back to our $100 investment but make the annual return $50 (or a 50% ROI). If you receive $50 every year it will take two years to cover your $100 investment, making your Payback Period two years. So, the calculation is total investment ($100) divided by annual return per year ($50) for two years. Simple.

At Nucleus, we believe Payback Period is the strongest metric you can use when proposing a technology initiative. In the two decades of delivering business cases and working with both sales teams and internal champions we've found it's easier to "feel" Payback Period than understand ROI. If you present the business case by stating that you expect the project to "cover its investment within the first 24 months," it's easier to grasp than saying the project has a 50% ROI. Of course, you need to use both metrics, but leading with Payback Period is a good strategy if you want to increase the likelihood that your project will be approved.

Payback Period is also a measure of risk. The longer a project takes to return its investment the more likely the returns you actually receive will vary from the initial estimates. Short payback periods make the naturally pessimistic finance types sleep easier at night because they know that if the worst happens, after the payback period, at least they've covered their cost.

Here Be Dragons

You can safely skip the rest of this if you'd like. There are only two metrics, Payback Period and ROI, and everything else is useless when assessing technology. Still reading? Okay then, we warned you.

Net Present Value (NPV) is the value today of money received at a future date. You probably already understand that $100 received today is worth more than $100 received a year from now. That's because you could put the $100 you receive today in the bank and get a return on that money. In our earlier example of the bank offering 5% on your $100 deposit, a year from now you'd get another $5 and have $105 total. So, getting $100 today to put in the bank is worth $5 more to you than $100 a year from now.

With NPV, we can bring the future payment back to today's money and calculate what the $100 you receive a year from now is worth today at a given interest rate, in this case 5%. We'll skip the actual formula and enter the numbers into a financial calculator to calculate an answer of $95.24. That means $100 a year from now has a "present value" of $95.24 today. Or, if you put $95.24 into the bank today at 5% interest rate you'll get $100 a year from now.

Okay, now this is where things get a bit more complex. Since you can calculate the present value of the money you receive a year from now, you can also calculate the present value of money received two, three, or more years from now. If you bring all those yearly values back to the present day, you can add them up and calculate the "Net Present Value" for the total project. You may have heard people ask, "what's the NPV of the project?" Adding the present value of all of the future payments is what they're talking about. But is NPV useful for assessing a technology project? Well, no, not at all. Let's look at the bank example. The bank offering a 5% rate on the $100 investment would return $5 each year, or $15 in the first three years. If we calculate the present value today of these future payments, we get $4.78 for the year-one payment, $4.54 for the year-two payment, and $4.32 for the year-three payment for a total NVP of these three payments of $13.64, not $15.00. That's the present value of the future payments, but when you calculate NPV you also need to include the initial cost. The math then becomes an initial outflow of $100 with net inflows of $13.64 for an actual NPV of a loss of $86.36.

"Wait, I lost money on this investment? I thought it has a 5% ROI?" It does, just a negative NPV in the first three years. We'd need to add back the residual value of the project at the end of year three (in this case it would be the $100 deposit) but that's impossible for a technology project with no residual value. We could go out further, to, say, year ten or twenty, but that isn't realistic and is just trying fix the underlying problem with the NPV metric. NPV is good for calculating the value of money at different periods in time, but adding it up and calculating the "Net" is only useful if the project has a defined beginning and end. That may be true if you're a construction company building an office building, but it isn't true with a technology investment delivering ongoing benefits.

The bottom line is that there's never a time when NPV can be used to assess a technology initiative.

Internal Rate of Return (IRR) is not ROI. If it were ROI it would be called ROI. It's not. Unfortunately, IRR has the word "return" in it so a lot of folks think it must be just as good as ROI. These people can be dangerous. The reality is IRR has nothing to do with the ROI of a project and calculates something completely different. IRR calculates the interest rate that sets the NPV stream equal to 0. Clear?

You might occasionally see IRR used as ROI in some technology vendor marketing material. Why? The obvious answer is that people don't know any better, but there's a more sinister answer that may be in play. An unscrupulous consultant can influence the IRR with very slight adjustments in the estimates of the benefits or the timeline, essentially creating the IRR you desire.

Let me show you how. Let's say I'm considering two projects that each require an initial investment of $100, and over the first ten years generate the same 100% IRR. Both projects appear equal and since I'm looking at a ten-year timeframe I can certainly make the case that I'm being thorough enough. But what if the first project returned $200 at the end of the first year and only $1 ten years later while the second project returned nothing for the first nine years and $102,000 in year ten? What—$102,000 in year ten?

Great! Clearly the second project is a lot better than the first. If we average the payments over the ten years and calculate average annual ROI, the first project has an annual ROI of 20 percent while the second has annual ROI of 10,200 percent.

Confused? Go back to the bank example. Imagine you and your friend each purchase a 10-year CD with a $100 investment offering a 100 percent IRR. Ten years later you walk in to the bank and they cheerfully give you $201 plus your initial $100 investment (and a pen) while your friend gets $102,000 plus their initial $100. You'll never see IRR used in banks. The problem is that if you extend the timeline and make minor adjustments early on in the payments, you can dramatically adjust the IRR. If we make the first project's initial payout $300 instead of $200, the IRR increases to 200 percent, making it appear twice as attractive as the second project, yet it's still a comparatively poor choice. Technically the issue is with the assumed reinvestment rate, and a formula called MIRR adjusts for that, but it's nothing more than an attempt to fix a bad metric.

I'd like to say we never see IRR but in fact our analysts see it on a regular basis. In one case we were asked to independently analyze an "ROI" business case generated by a vendor's business value team to justify the purchase of their solution by a large municipality. The business case was glowingly positive but when we assessed the benefits using ROI instead of the IRR calculation they used, we found the project would never generate a positive return. There was no way around it; the vendor was lying.

There are some very unique cases where IRR can be useful, but it's rare. The rule is to never use IRR to assess a technology investment. If you see it, or it's presented to you as a substitute for ROI, walk away.

Okay, still curious about IRR? Here's an example of how IRR can be used properly. Let's use our construction company example and assume that during the next year you plan to build a building. You make a detailed plan with the cost of materials and labor and the timings of the payments along with a final sale amount at the end of the project. Now you'll need to find a construction loan to pay for the project as you build it. Of course, the bank isn't going to negotiate with you on how much to give you. You need enough to build the building and half a building just won't do it. What the bank will negotiate on is the interest rate on the construction loan. Here's where IRR shines. IRR calculates the interest rate that sets the NPV equal to 0, thus leaving no money on the proverbial table. That's your table by the way. So, if you negotiate a rate with the bank that's less than the IRR you calculated there's extra money on that table for you. If the rate is higher than the IRR you're using your profits to add money to the table. Cool, right?

Total Cost of Ownership (TCO) is nothing more than the total cost of, well, ownership. It's a good number to understand but it only tells you the cheapest project, not the best, and the cheapest direction is always to do nothing. Calculating TCO is useful when budgeting for the cost side of a project but for the most part ignore TCO as a metric for making technology decisions.

Cost to Benefit Ratio calculates the return for every $1 spent. It's a useful metric for helping non-finance people understand the magnitude of an investment, but should be expressed as a 1 to X number rather than a percentage. We sometimes see ROI miscalculated as the total benefits over 3 years divided by the costs. That's really just the benefit to cost ratio, not ROI. It's not useful in any way.

There are other metrics, and plenty of people talking about opportunity costs or risk factors when assessing technology. You can safely ignore all of that. The only two metrics to use are Payback Period and ROI. They are tried and true, they got early cavemen out hunting, they are taught to every finance professional, and there's only one way to calculate them correctly.

Finance isn't trendy.

CASE STUDIES

SALESFORCE
FINANCIAL INSTITUTION

THE BOTTOM LINE

A financial services firm upgraded Salesforce Marketing Cloud and integrated it with Salesforce Service Cloud to streamline its marketing campaign process and ensure compliance with new regulatory requirements for financial advisors. Nucleus found that the upgrade project enabled the company to modernize its client and participant communications, ensure compliance, and increase client service and marketing productivity, reducing the time to prepare a campaign from weeks to days. The company was also able to avoid the one-time cost of communicating new information to clients by digitizing the process.

- ROI: 656%
- Payback: 3 Weeks

THE COMPANY

The financial services firm profiled in this case study is a privately held global company providing financial services including investment and wealth management, retirement services, life insurance, and mutual funds. The multibillion-dollar company provides retirement savings plans, executive compensation and stock plans, and health and other benefits management services as part of its solutions for employers.

THE CHALLENGE

The company has been using Salesforce since 2010, and the division providing solutions for employers implemented Salesforce Service Cloud and ExactTarget — which was later acquired by Salesforce and became Salesforce Marketing Cloud — in 2014. As is not unusual, both clouds were purchased separately and operated independently, with Service Cloud and Marketing Cloud running as separate applications in the sales and marketing departments, respectively.

When the marketing operations team wanted to launch a new campaign, it had to go to Salesforce Service Cloud to create and download a campaign list, send the list to sales and service representatives to validate each client's status, and then reload the finalized list into the Salesforce Marketing Cloud. As a result, typical time to launch a basic marketing campaign was four weeks.

To further complicate the process, in April 2016 the U.S. Department of Labor (DOL) issued a rule under the Employee Retirement Income Security Act of 1974 (ERISA) expanding the role of financial advisors overseeing retirement accounts to that of a fiduciary. This rule required the company to comply with a more stringent client-advisor relationship standard by January 1, 2018. To ensure compliance, the division needed an efficient way to confirm who was providing plan and participant advice for more than 20,000 clients and nearly 30 million plan participants. The marketing team recognized that it needed to streamline its processes to accelerate marketing communications and automate tracking to ensure that all client communication met the DOL requirements.

THE STRATEGY

The company decided that an upgrade and integration would be the best approach to solve both its marketing productivity and compliance challenges. The division worked with Salesforce's professional services team in Nomber 2016 to synchronize the data from Service Cloud and Marketing Cloud and to upgrade to the 2016 Winter release of Salesforce Marketing Cloud — which took approximately six weeks. The services also included knowledge transfer, which was critical to helping the team understand how to best leverage Journey Builder.

Additionally, the company invested in a marketing and communications campaign to inform its clients and their employees about the new communication channel.

Now, data is automatically synchronized between Service Cloud and Marketing Cloud, and marketing campaign list approval and management is automated through Salesforce Campaigns. The team continues to use Salesforce professional services on an ongoing basis to supplement their efforts as their marketing and communication volumes continue to grow.

KEY BENEFIT AREAS

With the help of Salesforce Marketing Cloud's professional services team, the division automated its marketing campaign process and launched digital client response tracking. Key benefits achieved include:

- **Increased client engagement.** The company replaced infrequent "batch-and-blast campaigns with automated, customized campaign journeys—increasing client engagement as well as campaign response rates.
- **Reduced paper and postage costs.** Updating processes enabled the company to onboard new clients and manage existing clients digitally while ensuring compliance—eliminating the printing and postage costs associated with traditional mailings.
- **Increased productivity.** Automating data synchronization and management has eliminated manual processes and significantly reduced the processing time for new client onboarding and marketing campaign approvals.
- **Reduced regulatory risk.** Digital tracking enables the company to efficiently ensure compliance under the new DOL rule, including Advice Amendment and Fiduciary Confirmation.

KEY COST AREAS

The company was able to leverage its existing Salesforce licenses, so no additional software costs were incurred. Costs of the project included consulting costs for implementation and ongoing management and optimization, personnel time to implement the application, and the cost of marketing campaigns to educate clients on the new processes.

LESSONS LEARNED

The company saw the new regulatory requirements as an opportunity to streamline its marketing campaign process and make client service more efficient. Because this resulted in significant cost and productivity savings, the company is now changing the way it invests in educational processes both internally and externally to further differentiate its services for both clients and clients' employees.

This case study is an example of how Salesforce customers are increasingly leveraging its technologies to support business-to-business and business-to-business-to-consumer requirements in digital transformation. Because ultimately user acceptance and adoption is critical to success, the company needed to include an investment in marketing—both at the traditional level, to its clients, and at a broader level, to its clients' employees who were ultimately impacted—to ensure the transition to digital communications was successful.

It is also representative of the evolution Nucleus sees in many Salesforce customers who initially invested in separate clouds to support sales, marketing, service, and other functions. As they see the benefits of providing a streamlined view of customer data across sales, marketing, and service, Nucleus expects they will increase investments in areas such as data mapping and Salesforce Customer 360 to maximize return from their cloud CRM investments.

CALCULATING THE ROI

Nucleus quantified the initial and ongoing costs of consulting, personnel time to implement the application, and marketing campaign costs over a 3-year period to calculate the company's total investment in the project. Because the company was able to use its existing Salesforce licenses, there was no additional incremental Salesforce license subscription fee.

Direct benefits quantified included the elimination of paper mailings based on the cost of postage per letter sent. The indirect benefits quantified included time saved on digital forms and time saved on confirming compliance. These productivity savings were quantified based on the average annual fully loaded cost of an employee using a correction factor for the inefficient transfer between time saved and additional time worked.

Not quantified in this analysis were the additional benefits the company will achieve by having a more integrated view of its clients and clients' employees, and the ability to more rapidly respond to market and regulatory changes.

Financial Analysis

Annual ROI: 656% • Payback Period: 0.1 years

Benefits	Pre-Start	Year 1	Year 2	Year 3
Direct	0	7,360,000	0	0
Indirect	0	5,261,538	213,462	213,462
Total per period	**0**	**12,621,538**	**213,462**	**213,462**

Costs—Capitalized Assets	Pre-Start	Year 1	Year 2	Year 3
Software	0	0	0	0
Hardware	0	0	0	0
Project consulting & personnel	0	0	0	0
Total per period	**0**	**0**	**0**	**0**

Costs—Depreciation	Pre-Start	Year 1	Year 2	Year 3
Software	0	0	0	0
Hardware	0	0	0	0
Project consulting & personnel	0	0	0	0
Total per period	**0**	**0**	**0**	**0**

Costs—Depreciation	Pre-Start	Year 1	Year 2	Year 3
Software	0	0	0	0
Hardware	0	0	0	0
Consulting	27,000	123,000	123,000	123,000
Personnel	36,000	0	0	0
Training	0	0	0	0
Other	581,603	0	0	0
Total per period	**644,603**	**123,000**	**123,000**	**123,000**

Financial Analysis	Results	Year 1	Year 2	Year 3
All government taxes	45%			
Cost of capital	7.0%			
Net cash flow before taxes	(644,603)	12,498,538	90,462	90,462
Net cash flow after taxes	(354,532)	6,874,196	49,754	49,754
Annual ROI: direct & indirect benefits				**656%**
Annual ROI: direct benefits only				362%
Net Present Value (NPV)				6,154,022
Payback period				**0.1 years**
Average Annual Cost of Ownership				337,868
3-Year IRR				1840%

All calculations are based on Nucleus Research's independent analysis of the expected costs and benefits associated with the solution.

SALESFORCE
SEQUOIA FINANCIAL GROUP

THE BOTTOM LINE

Sequoia Financial Group, LLC deployed Salesforce Financial Services Cloud to modernize its customer relationship management (CRM) solution and help serve more clients at scale. The company pivoted from custom task-based processes to repeatable case-based processes to streamline efforts and standardize the documentation of customer information. On average, the team of 65 users saves 0.8 hours each, daily, from the improvements enabled by Financial Services Cloud. Additionally, the company was able to avoid hiring an additional full-time equivalent (FTE) as well as simplify its information technology (IT) ecosystem by transitioning off Microsoft Dynamics and reducing costs associated with an additional CRM solution.

- ROI: 188%
- Payback: 1 Year

THE COMPANY

Sequoia Financial Group, LLC (Sequoia, Sequoia Financial), provides financial advisory services for business owners, retirees, young professionals, and high-net-worth private clients. It also offers asset management, wealth planning, insurance, and other institutional services. Founded in 1991, the firm is based in Akron, Ohio, with locations in Ohio, Michigan, and Florida.

THE CHALLENGE

In 2008, Sequoia started using Microsoft Dynamics to handle its CRM needs. However, in early 2017 they performed a client segmentation project that resulted in the need to modernize their existing solution to serve more clients at scale. The company leaders realized that a new solution to track client interactions and equip managers with relevant and contextual account information would increase customer satisfaction, allowing the organization to grow while controlling IT complexity.

Everything that Sequoia used in Microsoft Dynamics was task-based which meant that each item required manual typing to document and detail. This process was slow, resulting in variable data, and making standardization and analysis cumbersome.

The project team investigated different providers and systems, but these systems did not effectively integrate with Dynamics, requiring extensive consulting and custom configuration to deliver all the needed functionality. However, when the project team researched Salesforce Financial Services Cloud, they found that it offered all the necessary functionality out-of-the-box.

THE STRATEGY

The implementation of Financial Services Cloud took approximately nine months from the beginning of September 2017 to the go-live in April 2018. An internal project team from Sequoia worked with implementation consultants from NextGen Consulting Group, to implement and configure the solution. Resources equivalent to one full-time IT agent are used to support the system on an ongoing basis. Maintenance largely consists of handling feature requests and resolving issues for users. AppExchange solutions enhance the required processes by reducing the amount of custom configuration needed to meet functionality demands.

A team of 65 users was trained to use Financial Services Cloud for approximately six hours. Training was conducted by classroom-style and pre-recorded online sessions that could be watched on-demand. Since the go-live, the company has added 25 new users to the system and anticipates an additional 15 percent increase in user count moving forward.

One key goal of the project was to improve the user interface and greatly reduce toggling between multiple screens to enter information as was the case with Dynamics. Salesforce Financial Services Cloud changed the software system from being task-based to case-based, replacing the manual typing to document each task with pre-made templates for repeatable cases. These cases can be tracked in real time to show each team member involved, as well as case status and action items. Additionally, the team leveraged Lightning Components to make the page layouts more intuitive. They configured Einstein for data analysis and reporting for executives, and used an accounting tool to share data across the entire Salesforce ecosystem.

KEY BENEFIT AREAS

Key benefit areas resulting from the Financial Services Cloud deployment included cost savings from reduced additional headcount, increased user productivity, and eliminated legacy software subscriptions.

- **Reduced additional headcount.** With the use of templates instead of manual typing to document cases, users are able to serve a greater number of customers without additional resources. On the legacy Dynamics system, it would have required one additional hire of a full-time equivalent to reach the same level of service.
- **Increased productivity.** By eliminating multi-screen, click-through processes in favor of connected workflows and reusable templates, each of the 65 users saves on average 0.8 hours per day when compared to the legacy systems. This allows agents to spend more time on value-add tasks and less time navigating superfluous windows and performing administrative tasks.
- **Eliminated software subscriptions.** The deployment reduced Sequoia's overall IT complexity and it eliminated spend on Dynamics and another CRM solution. The deployment of Financial Services Cloud did not compromise functionality or interrupt operations.

KEY COST AREAS

The largest cost area of the Sequoia deployment were for third-party consulting and internal personnel executing the implementation. Other costs included software licenses and the training program to onboard new employees.

LESSONS LEARNED

This project highlights the benefit of choosing a solution that is purpose-built for a customer's industry. Sequoia Financial previously used Microsoft Dynamics, a generalized CRM system, and found that to customize it to include all requisite functionality would have taken over a year and incurred twice the implementation costs. Sequoia saw that Financial Services Cloud was built specifically for financial services use cases and it came with the needed functionality available out-of-the-box. Choosing an industry solution allowed Sequoia to bring their system live faster—in nine months as opposed to a year and a half—and reduced costly custom development.

NextGen Consulting, the implementation partner, was already familiar with the common uses and problems of financial services customers which helped further expedite the process. Using AppExchange solutions to fill gaps in core functionality instead of developing custom solutions was another best practice that Sequoia used to maximize its ROI. Leveraging the AppExchange and its thousands of partner-built solutions, Sequoia found currently available solutions instead of spending time and money developing similar functionality. It leveraged Tamarac and an integration with Schwab for portfolio management and increased visibility to customer assets. The company also deployed AccountingSeed for use as a general ledger and integrated resource planning tool.

CALCULATING THE ROI

Nucleus Research analyzed the costs of software, hardware, personnel, professional services, and user training over a three-year period to determine Sequoia Financial's total investment in Salesforce technology. Direct and indirect benefits were also quantified over the three-year period.

Direct benefits included the cost savings from the eliminated software expenditures and the reduced additional headcount of one full-time equivalent worker. Indirect benefits included the time savings that each user experienced as a result of workflow improvements and using pre-made templates to log cases. We calculated the time-savings benefit using the fully loaded cost per hour of employees. Time savings were multiplied by a correction factor to account for the inefficient transfer of time between time saved and additional time worked.

Financial Analysis

Annual ROI: 188% • Payback Period: 1.0 years

Benefits	Pre-Start	Year 1	Year 2	Year 3
Direct	0	223,240	256,726	295,235
Indirect	0	631,703	911,670	1,528,331
Total per period	**0**	**854,943**	**1,168,396**	**1,823,566**

Costs—Capitalized Assets	Pre-Start	Year 1	Year 2	Year 3
Software	36,028	0	0	0
Hardware	0	0	0	0
Project consulting & personnel	197,300	0	0	0
Total per period	**233,328**	**0**	**0**	**0**

Costs—Depreciation	Pre-Start	Year 1	Year 2	Year 3
Software	0	7,206	7,206	0
Hardware	0	0	0	0
Project consulting & personnel	0	39,460	39,460	39,460
Total per period	**0**	**46,666**	**46,666**	**39,460**

Costs—Depreciation	Pre-Start	Year 1	Year 2	Year 3
Software	0	96,542	96,542	0
Hardware	0	0	0	0
Consulting	77,487	59,733	62,720	72,128
Personnel	24,282	175,000	187,500	72,128
Training	24,180	12,090	16,740	0
Other	0	0	0	0
Total per period	**125,949**	**343,365**	**363,502**	**144,255**

Financial Analysis	Results	Year 1	Year 2	Year 3
All government taxes	45%			
Cost of capital	7.0%			
Net cash flow before taxes	(359,277)	511,577	804,894	1,679,310
Net cash flow after taxes	(302,600)	302,367	463,691	941,378
Annual ROI: direct & indirect benefits				**188%**
Annual ROI: direct benefits only				2%
Net Present Value (NPV)				1,153,436
Payback period				**1.0 years**
Average Annual Cost of Ownership				403,467
3-Year IRR				127%

All calculations are based on Nucleus Research's independent analysis of the expected costs and benefits associated with the solution.

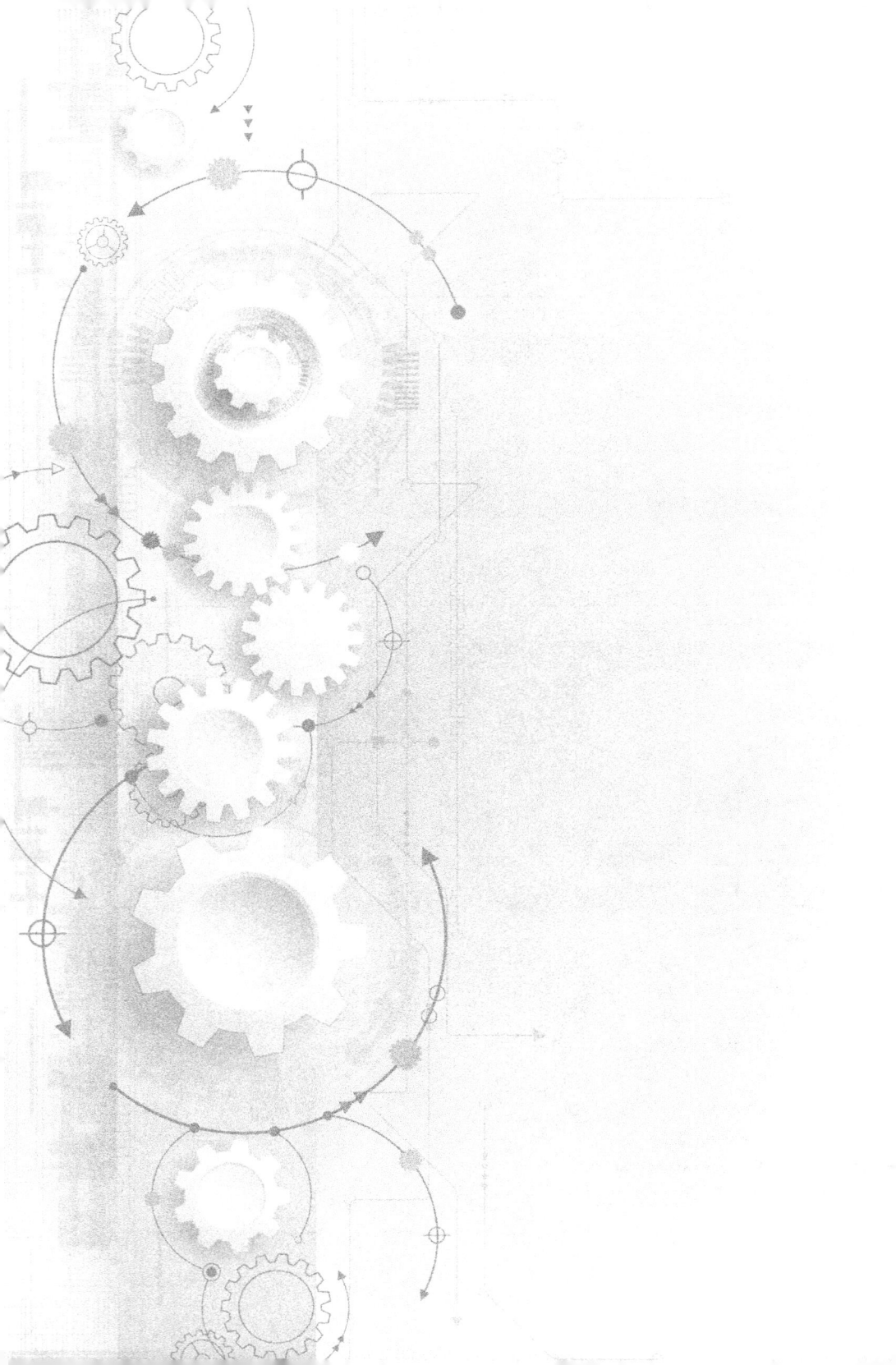

SALESFORCE
MATOUK

THE BOTTOM LINE

Matouk moved to Salesforce and Rootstock to modernize the management of its manufacturing business, from customer interactions to inventory and shop floor management. Nucleus found that the integrated customer relationship management (CRM) and enterprise resource planning (ERP) project enabled Matouk to drive greater visibility and productivity across all facets of its business. Accelerating time to promise and accuracy of quotes drove increased order volumes, supporting year-on-year growth of more than 10 percent while improving margins and customer satisfaction.

- ROI: 223%
- Payback: 6 Months
- Average Annual Benefits: $1,643,367

THE COMPANY

Matouk is a multi-generational, family-owned, high-end bedding and bath textile manufacturer based in Fall River, Massachusetts. With more than 100 employees, Matouk does most of its manufacturing under one roof at its factory, also located in Fall River.

THE CHALLENGE

Before implementing Salesforce and Rootstock, Matouk was using multiple applications to manage its business including an on-premise system and a homegrown Microsoft Access database. This technology strategy presented challenges for sales, marketing, service, and finance and operations, as they didn't have a common view or means to share information about customers and inventory. Additionally, the systems and data couldn't be accessed remotely or through a mobile application, meaning that all sharing and updating of data had to be done in the office.

Given the obvious challenges facing textiles manufacturers in North America, Matouk needed technology that would enable it to more nimbly compete on price, service, and ability to promise than its overseas and Internet-based competitors.

THE STRATEGY

Matouk began considering a new technology strategy in 2014, recognizing that it needed both a modern ERP solution for finance and manufacturing operations and a modern CRM solution to differentiate its sales and service to customers. The company considered a number of vendors including Microsoft, NetSuite, and Financial Force, and ultimately selected Salesforce and Rootstock (a Salesforce-native ERP solution) for the following reasons:

- Matouk had already completed a pilot of Salesforce in its sales and marketing departments, so it knew it could meet its users' needs and create less disruption than standardizing on a different CRM solution.
- Matouk recognized the value of using Salesforce Community Cloud as a way for customers to interact and didn't see a comparative solution available from other vendors.
- Rootstock was Salesforce native and had the cloud manufacturing ERP and manufacturing resource planning (MRP) capabilities Matouk needed to manage its warehouse, finance, and manufacturing operations.

The company made the decision in February 2015 and worked with Mountainpoint, a Salesforce and Rootstock consulting partner, to plan and deploy the two solutions. Given the transformative nature of the project and the integration and change management efforts, Matouk took a phased approach to its deployment, which spanned approximately 24 months and also included the use of Jitterbit for integration, Conga for contract management, and Zenkraft for shipping automation.

KEY BENEFIT AREAS

Moving to a cloud-based, integrated ERP and CRM environment has enabled Matouk to modernize its business and become nimbler so it can more effectively compete against both larger and smaller domestic and international competitors. Key benefits of the project include:

- **Improved technology management.** Matouk was able to eliminate the time and cost of supporting its old system as well as the investments that would have been needed to build custom integrations and analytics and reporting to give it the visibility it needed to be competitive.
- **Increased manufacturing staff productivity.** Increased automation and controls have enabled Matouk to optimize its manufacturing processes, enabling the company to increase output without a corresponding increase in manufacturing staff.
- **Increased warehouse productivity.** The mobile application has made it much easier to track goods from floor to finish. Before, workers never had work center-level visibility into how things were manufactured, and no idea of what was on the shop floor. Greater automation and visibility, as well as integrating shipping automation, has enabled Matouk to maintain the same level of warehouse staff while increasing shipping volumes.
- **Increased customer service productivity.** Matouk has been able to leverage Salesforce Community Cloud to provide self service to customers, reducing the burden on internal customer service staff while accelerating issue resolution.
- **Increased marketing productivity.** Access to marketing automation capabilities has enabled Matouk to increase the volume and sophistication of its electronic marketing campaigns with the same number of staff.
- **Increased visibility.** Before Salesforce and Rootstock, Matouk had limited visibility into key business indicators, like per-SKU

profitability, that could enable it to make business decisions that maximized profits. Today, integrated systems and analytics enable better visibility for both strategic product decisions and tactical activities like the generation of quotes based on stock availability.

- **Reduced inventory carrying costs.** Greater visibility enables Matouk to much better understand what it needs to hold for safety stock, meaning it can reduce inventory carrying costs, while also allowing for the ability to fill orders quickly. Although this has a small impact in terms of savings in working capital, for a SMB it frees up capital that was otherwise unavailable to pursue other growth opportunities.
- **Reduced shrinkage.** Greater visibility at a granular level into raw materials and inventory at every stage of the manufacturing process—and employee knowledge that this visibility exists—has enabled Matouk to reduce shrinkage by an estimated $100,000 per year.
- **Accelerated quote to cash.** Manufacturing has also been able to cut its lead time from six to four weeks, as products move faster into the system.

KEY COST AREAS

Costs of the project included software subscription, hardware (including iPads and scanners for the warehouse), consulting, personnel time to implement and support the application, and employee training time.

LESSONS LEARNED

Given the data-intensive nature of Matouk's project, it had to carefully consider data limits in Salesforce, and addressing data limits was a key reason for choosing Rootstock, because it would present a much small data footprint than some other Salesforce-native ERP solutions.

CALCULATING THE ROI

Nucleus quantified the initial and ongoing costs of software subscription fees, hardware, personnel time to implement the application, employee training time, and consulting over a 3-year period to calculate Matouk's total investment in Salesforce and Rootstock.

Direct benefits quantified included reduced support cost by retiring systems and elimination of server maintenance, as well as avoided cost of custom integrations and associated consulting. Matouk was also able to grow its manufacturing and warehouse operations while avoiding the need for additional hires, also a direct benefit. Direct business benefits also included reduced shrinkage.

The indirect benefits quantified increases in marketing and customer service productivity, based on the average annual fully loaded cost of an employee using a correction factor to account for the inefficient transfer between time saved and additional time worked. Additional indirect benefits quantified included change in working capital and increased profits driven by faster time to promise and more accurate quoting.

Salesforce: Building the ROI Business Case

Financial Analysis

Annual ROI: 223% • Payback Period: 0.5 years

Benefits	Pre-Start	Year 1	Year 2	Year 3
Direct	0	497,938	548,875	548,875
Indirect	0	1,037,843	1,148,286	1,148,286
Total per period	**0**	**1,535,780**	**1,697,161**	**1,697,161**

Costs—Capitalized Assets	Pre-Start	Year 1	Year 2	Year 3
Software	0	0	0	0
Hardware	0	0	0	0
Project consulting & personnel	0	0	0	0
Total per period	**0**	**0**	**0**	**0**

Costs—Depreciation	Pre-Start	Year 1	Year 2	Year 3
Software	0	0	0	0
Hardware	0	0	0	0
Project consulting & personnel	0	0	0	0
Total per period	**0**	**0**	**0**	**0**

Costs—Depreciation	Pre-Start	Year 1	Year 2	Year 3
Software	134,200	134,200	134,200	0
Hardware	7,100	0	0	0
Consulting	195,000	75,000	50,000	25,000
Personnel	263,925	103,240	103,240	103,240
Training	27,389	0	0	0
Other	0	0	0	0
Total per period	**627,614**	**312,440**	**287,440**	**128,240**

Financial Analysis	Results	Year 1	Year 2	Year 3
All government taxes	45%			
Cost of capital	7.0%			
Net cash flow before taxes	(627,614)	1,223,340	1,409,721	1,568,921
Net cash flow after taxes	(345,188)	672,837	775,346	862,906
Annual ROI: direct & indirect benefits				**223%**
Annual ROI: direct benefits only				46%
Net Present Value (NPV)				1,665,238
Payback period				**0.5 years**
Average Annual Cost of Ownership				451,912
3-Year IRR				198%

All calculations are based on Nucleus Research's independent analysis of the expected costs and benefits associated with the solution.

SALESFORCE
ICS+

THE BOTTOM LINE

ICS+ deployed Salesforce Sales Cloud, Service Cloud, Community Cloud, Quip, and Inbox, to provide one integrated platform for all client-focused data and collaboration. Moving from NetSuite, e-mail, and a variety of spreadsheets and other tools enabled the company to streamline project management, increase data capture and collaboration, increase employee productivity, and accelerate collections by one-third while increasing client satisfaction.

- ROI: 942%
- Payback: 6 Weeks
- Average Annual Benefits: $185,663

THE COMPANY

ICS+ specializes in building automation control systems, specializing in audio and video solutions for commercial properties such as hospitals, hotels, airports, and educational institutions, and for some large residential estates. Headquartered in Austin, TX, the company has been in business more than 10 years, growing as demand for custom video and audio installations in commercial properties has increased. Although the company has fewer than 10 employees, it completes roughly 100 to 115 client engagements each year.

THE CHALLENGE

Because ICS+ creates custom solutions for each customer, it also creates custom billing for each of its clients. Although the company had NetSuite for enterprise resource planning (ERP) and an existing customer relationship management (CRM) application, most of its project management and custom billing was handled manually or in spreadsheets, with collaboration and information sharing on different projects mostly happening through e-mail. This made it difficult for the company to have a complete view of project status across its client base and was a drain on productivity for sales, project managers, and accounting who didn't have a single source of updated information on client projects.

The company sought a solution that would provide it with an integrated view of client data across the sales and delivery lifecycle, and one that would have the flexibility to enable it to make changes over time as its business changed without the need to bring in external consultants.

THE STRATEGY

ICS+ began considering a number of new CRM options in 2014 and ultimately selected Salesforce for two main reasons:

- **Functionality.** In reviewing Salesforce's capabilities across clouds as well as add-ons available from partners, the company knew that Salesforce could meet its somewhat unique needs.
- **Integrated collaboration.** The capabilities of Salesforce Chatter and Quip would enable ICS+ to use Salesforce as its customer system of record by keeping all client-related communication and collaboration within the same application.

ICS+ took advantage of Salesforce's Premier Success services, which enabled the company to accelerate its deployment. It started with Employee Apps, then added Customer Community, Salesforce CPQ, Quip for collaboration, and Salesforce Inbox. The company also took advantage of strategy consulting and implementation services from Cloud Co-Op, a Salesforce partner. The internal team created its own training and users had an initial 2-day training session. Ongoing training sessions are held to introduce new capabilities. The initial rollout was completed by August 2015, and the company continues to extend its use of Salesforce functionality and partner capabilities, recently adding e-signature.

KEY BENEFIT AREAS

Deploying Salesforce has enabled ICS+ to continue to grow its business while improving its margins by having greater visibility into day-to-day operations. Key benefits of the project included:

- **Increased productivity.** Integration of quip with Salesforce and providing clients with access to Quip has reduced the amount of e-mail traffic by an average of 20 percent, with more precise details being captured within one system of record.
- **Improved technology management.** Moving from NetSuite enabled the company to significantly reduce its annual software license subscription fees while reducing the overall time needed to support technology.
- **Change in working capital.** Because of more timely and accurate project management data within Salesforce, ICS+ can invoice and collect from customers faster, shortening its accounts receivables cycle by 15 days.
- **Increased sales.** Tracking opportunities within Salesforce has enabled the company to track and close jobs better so it can both be more selective about opportunities it wants to pursue and close more deals.

KEY COST AREAS

Costs of the project included annual software subscription fees, initial and ongoing personnel time to deploy and support Salesforce, training time, and external consulting costs which ICS+ uses on an ongoing basis as needed.

LESSONS LEARNED

The low code and no code capabilities of Salesforce were an important factor in enabling ICS+ to make ongoing changes to its Salesforce footprint as its business needs evolved. Although the company has used some consulting services, it is able to perform many enhancements and custom modifications without the cost of outside help that was always needed when modifications to NetSuite needed to be made. It has also been able to leverage the Salesforce Success Community as a resource for support.

CALCULATING THE ROI

Nucleus quantified the initial and ongoing costs of software subscription fees, consulting costs, personnel time, and time spent in training to quantify ICS+'s total investment in Salesforce.

Direct benefits quantified included the elimination of NetSuite license subscription fees and the elimination of both internal time and consultant's fees that were associated with supporting NetSuite. Indirect benefits quantified included the increase in productivity for sales, service, and administrative staff as well as the increase in productivity across the board as a result of Quip.

These benefits were quantified based on the average annual fully loaded cost of the employees using productivity factor to account for the inefficient transfer of time between time saved and additional time worked. To avoid double counting, not included in the calculation were the increase in profits resulting from both increased revenues and improved margins driven by more effective opportunities, sales, and project tracking.

Salesforce: ICS+

Financial Analysis

Annual ROI: 942% • Payback Period: 0.1 years

Benefits	Pre-Start	Year 1	Year 2	Year 3
Direct	0	140,694	140,694	140,694
Indirect	0	44,968	44,968	44,968
Total per period	**0**	**185,663**	**185,663**	**185,663**

Costs—Capitalized Assets	Pre-Start	Year 1	Year 2	Year 3
Software	0	0	0	0
Hardware	0	0	0	0
Project consulting & personnel	0	0	0	0
Total per period	**0**	**0**	**0**	**0**

Costs—Depreciation	Pre-Start	Year 1	Year 2	Year 3
Software	0	0	0	0
Hardware	0	0	0	0
Project consulting & personnel	0	0	0	0
Total per period	**0**	**0**	**0**	**0**

Costs—Depreciation	Pre-Start	Year 1	Year 2	Year 3
Software	8,908	16,566	16,566	0
Hardware	0	0	0	0
Consulting	0	2,500	2,000	4,500
Personnel	1,217	27,000	23,625	23,625
Training	5,192	2,596	2,596	2,596
Other	0	0	0	0
Total per period	**15,317**	**48,662**	**44,787**	**30,721**

Financial Analysis	Results	Year 1	Year 2	Year 3
All government taxes	45%			
Cost of capital	7.0%			
Net cash flow before taxes	(15,317)	137,000	140,875	154,941
Net cash flow after taxes	(8,424)	75,350	77,481	85,218
Annual ROI: direct & indirect benefits				942%
Annual ROI: direct benefits only				648%
Net Present Value (NPV)				199,235
Payback period				**0.1 years**
Average Annual Cost of Ownership				46,496
3-Year IRR				897%

All calculations are based on Nucleus Research's independent analysis of the expected costs and benefits associated with the solution.

SALESFORCE QUIP
FINANCIAL SERVICES

THE BOTTOM LINE

An anonymous global financial services and insurance company deployed the Salesforce Quip tool to replace a legacy system and Microsoft Excel spreadsheets used to support the communication needs of its sales, business, and technology areas. Moving to Quip enabled the enterprise to retire the old process, improve productivity, reduce the inefficiency of frequent meetings by 83 percent, and achieve an average annual benefit of $167,379.

- ROI: 695%
- Payback: 1 Month

THE COMPANY

The company is a global operation that offers warranty solutions with insurance protection plans and service contracts for automobiles, electronic devices, and appliances. It provides underwriting, claims administration, and marketing expertise to manufacturers and distributors, as well as specialty insurance products and services for financial institutions. The company helps U. S. automobile dealers with finance and insurance (F&I) products, reinsurance options and training.

THE CHALLENGE

The company did not have an efficient collaboration platform. It was using a combination of Excel spreadsheets, Confluence, Sharepoint, and the Office suite of tools that no longer effectively met the company's needs and speed of information. To ensure continued growth of the company, it needed to implement a user-friendly collaboration platform.

THE STRATEGY

In early 2016 the company looked at several options including Confluence, Slack, and Microsoft Teams. The company had experience with Salesforce as its CRM provider, and opted for Quip as the logical solution. Key factors in the selection of Quip were:

- **Usability.** The employee experience with the Salesforce user-interface (UI) demonstrated its ease of use, overcoming the objections voiced and ensured quicker user adoption. The company experienced a substantial increase of user adoption with Quip. Within the first four months of deployment, more than 400 users were working with Quip. On the average, 100 new users are being added to the platform each month.
- **Integration and support.** The company was satisfied with the support it already received from Salesforce and the ability to seamlessly integrate CRM with collaboration reduced training time and costs.
- **Scalability.** The company expects significant increases the user base. Any new or additional software had to be able to accommodate this volume of expansion.

At present, the company is using Quip for most of its collaborative and document management needs.

KEY BENEFIT AREAS

The deployment of Quip allowed the company to retire an inefficient legacy system and modernize its collaborative efforts. Key benefits of the project included:

- **Reduced costs.** The company was able to eliminate the cost of its prior collaboration tools and modernize its workflow processes, reducing the number of meetings and saving the company more than $150,000 annually.
- **Improved productivity.** The average user previously had to search an average of six to seven sites to collect data needed for analysis and proposals. Now, users can locate necessary information from a single source, thereby reducing "look" times significantly.
- **Improved efficiency.** Meetings, in lieu of an efficient collaboration tool, were costing the company time and money. On the average, 18 meeting were held per week involving 4 or more staff and lasting one and a half hours each. With Quip, physical meetings were reduced to less than three per week and the collaborative sessions were far shorter, leading to better results.

KEY COST AREAS

Most of the costs associated with the deployment of Quip are annual product licensing fees representing more than 95 percent of the total cost. Training is taking less than 15 minutes per user due to the intuitive nature of the tool. Other cost areas extrapolated over the three-year period included minimal initial and ongoing personnel costs to implement and support the solution.

LESSONS LEARNED

The company did require a lot of evaluation to define its collaboration needs. It knew that the existing combination of Excel spreadsheets, SharePoint, and Confluence were inadequate, and it wanted a tool that would integrate with its Salesforce CRM platform. The company recognized that user adoption would be a challenge since earlier tools were rejected by the staff, and knew it needed an internal transition strategy that included both user training and management support. The company's advice to other companies looking for a collaboration tool was to keep it simple as possible and involve users early in the process.

CALCULATING THE ROI

To calculate the company's total investment in Quip, Nucleus quantified the initial and ongo-ing costs over a three-year period for software, personnel, and training. Direct benefits quan-tified included the cost savings from the retirement of the legacy program. Indirect benefits included improved productivity and efficiency. The company believes that the unified platform will offer additional benefits as Quip and Salesforce expand their offerings.

Financial Analysis

Annual ROI: 695% • Payback Period: 0.1 years

Benefits	Pre-Start	Year 1	Year 2	Year 3
Direct	0	0	0	0
Indirect	0	167,379	167,379	167,379
Total per period	**0**	**167,379**	**167,379**	**167,379**

Costs—Capitalized Assets	Pre-Start	Year 1	Year 2	Year 3
Software	0	0	0	0
Hardware	0	0	0	0
Project consulting & personnel	0	0	0	0
Total per period	**0**	**0**	**0**	**0**

Costs—Depreciation	Pre-Start	Year 1	Year 2	Year 3
Software	0	0	0	0
Hardware	0	0	0	0
Project consulting & personnel	0	0	0	0
Total per period	**0**	**0**	**0**	**0**

Costs—Depreciation	Pre-Start	Year 1	Year 2	Year 3
Software	0	72,000	144,000	144,000
Hardware	0	0	0	0
Consulting	0	0	0	0
Personnel	4,754	8,910	8,910	8,910
Training	0	4,868	4,077	7,302
Other	0	0	0	0
Total per period	**4,754**	**85,778**	**156,987**	**160,212**

Financial Analysis	Results	Year 1	Year 2	Year 3
All government taxes	45%			
Cost of capital	7.0%			
Net cash flow before taxes	(4,754)	81,601	10,392	7,167
Net cash flow after taxes	(2,614)	44,881	5,716	3,942
Annual ROI: direct & indirect benefits				**695%**
Annual ROI: direct benefits only				-2826%
Net Present Value (NPV)				47,540
Payback period				**0.1 years**
Average Annual Cost of Ownership				135,910
3-Year IRR				1630%

All calculations are based on Nucleus Research's independent analysis of the expected costs and benefits associated with the solution.

SALESFORCE
VVMWARE INC.

THE BOTTOM LINE

VMWare Inc. (VMW) deployed Salesforce Pardot, Marketing Cloud, and Sales Cloud to facilitate a new business-to-business (B2B) marketing strategy for its cloud portfolio, and to integrate its marketing data with sales to produce a more unified customer view. The project enabled VMW to increase user productivity, accelerate campaign launch times from months to weeks, and increase profits through improved lead generation and conversion.

- ROI: 641%
- Payback: 2.4 Months

THE COMPANY

VMW is a publicly-traded subsidiary of Dell Technologies, based out of Palo Alto, California, with over 120 locations and 20,000 employees worldwide. Founded in 1998, VMW was acquired by EMC Corporation in 2004 (which Dell acquired in 2016) for its platform virtualization capabilities. It continues to develop and sell cloud computing and virtualization products with the aim of separating application software from its underlying hardware to create a flexible digital foundation to support businesses.

THE CHALLENGE

VMW has leveraged digital marketing for many years, designing and executing ad campaigns with a composite on-premise solution built on legacy systems integrated with a set of custom tools. Within this framework, each campaign took six months on average to complete and overall marketing agility was handicapped.

Additionally, the legacy system didn't support marketing-sales integration, lacking key functionality such as lead scoring and prioritization. VMW understood that to sustain continued growth, it needed to modernize sales and marketing reporting.

THE STRATEGY

A large-scale update to the legacy system was proposed, but after defining the project goals it became apparent that migrating to a new cloud-based solution was more feasible and conducive to long-term growth. Along with the platform transition, VMW was reformulating its marketing approach to a cloud-based B2B strategy and this was considered when selecting the appropriate platform. Salesforce was the only provider seriously considered for the following reasons:

- **B2B Focus.** Salesforce Pardot is a cloud-based marketing automation solution built to design, deploy, analyze, and manage B2B advertisement campaigns.
- **Creation and integration of custom apps.** Additional apps can be easily created within the Salesforce ecosystem, eliminating integration complications and reducing the time required from feature request to rollout.
- **Salesforce relationship.** The parent company, Dell, maintains a pre-existing enterprise agreement with Salesforce which VMW leveraged to achieve cost savings on the software subscriptions and licenses.

After officially deciding to move forward with Salesforce, a joint six-person Customer Success team was primarily responsible for implementing the new solution, an integrated environment of Pardot, Marketing Cloud, and Sales Cloud.

The project commenced in Spring 2017—initial setup lasted three and a half months until the official deployment in August 2017. No third-party consultants were used to configure the deployment—instead, the VP of Product Marketing and Cloud Solutions provided technical support. The agreement between Dell and Salesforce also includes ongoing personnel support to manage the system; an administrator works remotely from Brazil, and two operators work to develop and implement feature requests for users in order to custom-fit the software to the unique business processes of VMW. Both operators and the project team completed a two-day training module with Pardot to get familiar with the platform.

To date there are 15 users on the system with 11 power users (six members of the original project team with five new users). An additional 30 people can input data but don't have access to the on-platform tools. VMW currently actively manages 15-20 independent campaigns on the platform.

KEY BENEFIT AREAS

Deploying Salesforce Pardot, Marketing Cloud, and Sales Cloud together allowed VMW to modernize its sales and marketing strategy, decrease spending on IT support, and increase total sales. Overall agility was improved, and the company can now execute at speeds that were impossible on the legacy system, driving increases in productivity and profits. Key benefits of the project included:

- **Eliminated legacy system support costs.** Moving to Salesforce allowed VMW to retire legacy software and achieve savings from eliminated license fees. The simplicity of the new stack reduced the need for ongoing personnel support; subsequently one full-time IT staffer was redeployed.
- **Increased contributor productivity.** On-platform automation, the usability of the platform, and sales and marketing data unified on the Sales Cloud have increased contributor productivity by 20 percent. Automated data generation removes human error and improves data quality with Einstein Automated Contacts. On the legacy system, a single ad campaign took six months to build, while on Salesforce this is reduced to two and a half weeks.
- **Increased marketing effectiveness.** With the ability to turn out campaigns at a faster rate, VMW better able to segment and target the

right customers. With analytics capabilities from Salesforce Einstein embedded, teams can leverage sales, marketing, and customer data to sell more effectively. For lead generation, the project allowed VMW to market a cohesive message across all 17 products and services; in the first day of go-live, sales met and doubled its lead target for the month.

- **Additional revenue capture through marketing.** Centralizing all customer data allows users to perform lead-scoring and lead-prioritization and deliver the insights to sales teams. Marketers have access to recent sales data, allowing them to create customized campaigns to more effectively leverage account-based marketing. Twenty percent of additional revenues are attributed to the deployment.

KEY COST AREAS

The greatest cost area for the deployment was software expenses. The majority of this spending went toward Salesforce subscriptions, however the cost to license and build other solutions—Salesforce DMP, Lattice, and a number of custom apps—is also included. Other costs included initial and ongoing personnel support and the cost of user time spent in training.

LESSONS LEARNED

This case is a clear example of a multinational corporation identifying a sunk cost in an inefficient legacy system and embracing innovation on the cloud at the enterprise scale. VMW realized the need to integrate sales with marketing to facilitate the comprehensive customer understanding needed that drives sales in the modern marketplace. To reconfigure the legacy system would have been costly in personnel time and lost productivity, so investment in cloud innovation was the more feasible choice, particularly given the benefits to collaboration, data management, business agility, and total ROI that Nucleus has identified as characteristic to cloud deployments (Nucleus Research, r208—Cloud now delivers 3.2 times more ROI—December 2017).

Within VMW the deployment was smoothly executed, taking only three and a half months from start to finish. A crucial policy for companies undertaking a platform migration on this scale is to provide adequate training on the system in order to ensure end-user confidence and adoption.

CALCULATING THE ROI

To calculate VMW's total investment in Salesforce, Nucleus quantified the initial and ongoing costs over a three-year period for software, consulting, personnel, and training.

Direct benefits quantified include eliminated software license maintenance fees and the cost savings from a redeployed worker, calculated based on the average annual fully-loaded cost of the redeployed staff.

Indirect benefits quantified include additional revenue captured via the new marketing system applying an average profit margin, and increased contributor productivity, calculated using the average annual fully loaded cost of the affected staff and applying a correction factor to account for the inefficient transfer of time between time saved and additional time worked.

Financial Analysis

Annual ROI: 641% • Payback Period: 2.4 months

Benefits	Pre-Start	Year 1	Year 2	Year 3
Direct	0	300,000	300,000	300,000
Indirect	0	11,620,000	11,620,000	11,620,000
Total per period	**0**	**11,920,000**	**11,920,000**	**11,920,000**

Costs—Capitalized Assets	Pre-Start	Year 1	Year 2	Year 3
Software	0	0	0	0
Hardware	0	0	0	0
Project consulting & personnel	0	0	0	0
Total per period	**0**	**0**	**0**	**0**

Costs—Depreciation	Pre-Start	Year 1	Year 2	Year 3
Software	0	0	0	0
Hardware	0	0	0	0
Project consulting & personnel	0	0	0	0
Total per period	**0**	**0**	**0**	**0**

Costs—Depreciation	Pre-Start	Year 1	Year 2	Year 3
Software	1,200,000	1,200,000	1,200,000	0
Hardware	0	0	0	0
Consulting	0	0	0	0
Personnel	472,500	294,500	294,500	294,500
Training	16,615	0	0	0
Other	0	0	0	0
Total per period	**1,689,115**	**1,494,500**	**1,494,500**	**294,500**

Financial Analysis	Results	Year 1	Year 2	Year 3
All government taxes	45%			
Cost of capital	7.0%			
Net cash flow before taxes	(1,689,115)	10,425,500	10,425,500	11,625,500
Net cash flow after taxes	(929,013)	5,734,025	5,734,025	6,394,025
Annual ROI: direct & indirect benefits				**641%**
Annual ROI: direct benefits only				-47%
Net Present Value (NPV)				14,657,637
Payback period				**0.2 years**
Average Annual Cost of Ownership				1,657,538
3-Year IRR				617%

All calculations are based on Nucleus Research's independent analysis of the expected costs and benefits associated with the solution.

SALESFORCE
SUPERIOR POOL SPA AND LEISURE

THE BOTTOM LINE

Superior Pool Spa and Leisure, Ltd., deployed Salesforce Field Service Lightning (FSL) to address challenges with organization, communication, and efficiency associated with growing the business. The project enabled Superior to provide end-to-end visibility into its field service operations, improving customer satisfaction and internal communications. Superior has redeployed seven staff members while accelerating job resolution and increasing customer retention, earning the company an average of two new contracts per month.

- ROI: 157%
- Payback: 10 Months

THE COMPANY

Superior Pool, Spa and Leisure Ltd. was established in 1973 in Ontario, Canada, where it is a leader in commercial pool, spa, and recreation facility management. It manages over 300 indoor swimming and recreational facilities year-round, with at least 250 more in the summer months. Additionally, it operates year-round construction and service departments with field service staff servicing over 150 customers per day.

THE CHALLENGE

As Superior grew, it faced increasing difficulty coordinating work orders between dispatchers and field service staff. Compiling the completed and outstanding work orders was inefficient and error-prone as multiple databases were being used in conjunction to maintain business operations. Invoicing was difficult to standardize, and customers were beginning to grow frustrated with the overall variable wait-time between work request, completion, and billing.

To address these inefficiencies and support future growth, Superior needed a solution that could streamline operations by consolidating all processes — optimizing dispatching and scheduling, accessing customer service history, resolving cases — on one platform. A sister company utilized Sage for their needs, however after a test-period, Superior decided to explore other options. After considering Microsoft Dynamics, NetSuite, and Sage, it opted to go with Salesforce for the following reasons:

- **Scalability.** The Salesforce platform is easily scalable to accommodate company growth.
- **Integration with Sage and the greater Salesforce ecosystem.** Accounting data from Sage could be easily migrated to the platform, enabling it to become the centralized hub for company data.
- **Ease-of-use.** High usability increases the rate of adoption. Reliable mobile compatibility ensures that technicians in the field are equipped with the same tools as staff in the office.

THE STRATEGY

The team at Superior decided on FSL in August 2015 and they moved forward in September. The project started in October, with the team working with third-party consultants to migrate legacy data, map new processes and workflows, make needed upgrades to the company's enterprise resource planning (ERP) system and network, and plan and execute training.

Three technicians were trained early on the platform as "early adopters" to champion the solution and serve as a resource for other new users during adoption. To ensure full competency with the system prior to its full rollout, all users were trained on the system three separate times: the first session was a group session in-office, the second was hands-on manual training, and the third included a one-on-one session with each user.

Currently, FSL is used to dispatch the mobile workforce and enable them with real-time data on the job. Salesforce is now Superior's central hub for all their service needs. They can streamline operations by consolidating all processes—optimizing dispatching and scheduling, accessing customer service history, resolving cases—all on one platform. For technicians especially, Salesforce is a one-stop shop for all operations—from showing available appointments to managing routes to on-the-job clarity of what needs to be addressed—which helps them better plan their days, increase productivity, and function as an extension of the office.

Since deploying Salesforce, Superior is the only supplier operating with a fully connected, cloud-based customer service platform designed for aquatics and leisure management. The combination of this high-tech operating system and excellence in customer service positions Superior as the innovative leader in the industry.

KEY BENEFIT AREAS

Superior achieved a number of benefits from modernizing on Salesforce FSL, including enhanced visibility, greater efficiency, cost savings, and increased total revenue. The improvements centered around optimizing company resource allocation, in both labor and materials, leading to a greater number of service calls completed at a lower overall cost. The benefits included the following:

- **Redeployed staff.** Due to increased efficiency and productivity, Superior was able to redeploy 3 field service staff, 2 service technicians, 2 office staff, redistributing an increased workload across the remaining staff, and placing the reassigned staff in customer-facing roles.
- **Reduced logistics costs.** Due to the planning and visualization features of FSL, driver routes were optimized to reduce fuel costs.
- **Reduced technology costs.** Savings were achieved by eliminating legacy system licenses and support costs and integrating company data and operations to Salesforce.
- **Increased customer service focus on client satisfaction.** Eighty percent of service calls are now resolved within 24 hours, leading to 95 percent customer retention, shortening the average time until

resolution from 2 weeks to 1.6 days, and allowing Superior to offer 24-hour services.
- **Increased profits.** Profits have increased through new contracts and reduced customer churn.
- **Increased productivity.** With FSL, managers saved five hours of work per week that has been redirected to improve operations and grow the business.

KEY COST AREAS

Key cost areas of Superior's deployment of Salesforce FSL over the three-year period included software subscription costs, third-party consulting, personnel costs to implement the solution and train users, and user training time. The largest cost area of the deployment was the consulting, making up 38 percent of the total project.

BEST PRACTICES

No project of this size and complexity could have been accomplished without the commitment of the entire team, and the planning and deployment was a companywide effort. Seeing the benefits of modernizing with new technology, Superior's staff embraced the opportunity and, as a result, the company was able to replace six different programs with a single product that has provided each staff member with tools not previously available, allowing them to deliver significant improvements in customer service.

When undertaking a project of this nature, Superior also accurately identified the need for repetitive training on the system to ensure user adoption and competency. The three-phased training program included office-wide demos, early training for pilot users to champion the solution among their peers and serve as a resource for new users, and a one-on-one session with each individual to address user-specific barriers to entry.

CALCULATING THE ROI

Nucleus Research analyzed the costs of software, hardware, personnel, consulting, and training over a three-year period to quantify Superior Pool's investment in Salesforce. Direct and indirect benefits achieved as a result of the investment were also quantified over the three-year period.

Direct benefits quantified included eliminated technology costs from legacy systems, the fully-loaded cost of redeployed staff, and reduced logistics costs.

Indirect benefits included increased management productivity, increased profits, and increased customer service focus on client satisfaction. Indirect benefits were calculated using the fully loaded cost per hour of employees. Time savings were multiplied by a productivity factor to account for the inefficient transfer of time.

Benefits not quantified include improvements to company culture through increased individual accountability from analytics-based evaluations supported by the Salesforce platform, and increased field service worker retention due to greater employee satisfaction. This is likely to manifest in less turnover, resulting in lower onboarding costs and reduced productivity-losses from training new hires.

Financial Analysis

Annual ROI: 157% • Payback Period: 0.8 years

Benefits	Pre-Start	Year 1	Year 2	Year 3
Direct	0	799,000	799,000	799,000
Indirect	0	163,444	163,444	163,444
Total per period	**0**	**962,444**	**962,444**	**962,444**

Costs—Capitalized Assets	Pre-Start	Year 1	Year 2	Year 3
Software	0	0	0	0
Hardware	0	0	0	0
Project consulting & personnel	0	0	0	0
Total per period	**0**	**0**	**0**	**0**

Costs—Depreciation	Pre-Start	Year 1	Year 2	Year 3
Software	0	0	0	0
Hardware	0	0	0	0
Project consulting & personnel	0	0	0	0
Total per period	**0**	**0**	**0**	**0**

Costs—Depreciation	Pre-Start	Year 1	Year 2	Year 3
Software	82,800	82,800	82,800	0
Hardware	80,000	0	0	0
Consulting	180,000	240,000	60,000	60,000
Personnel	100,000	32,452	32,452	32,452
Training	37,320	0	0	0
Other	0	500	500	500
Total per period	**480,120**	**355,752**	**175,752**	**92,952**

Financial Analysis	Results	Year 1	Year 2	Year 3
All government taxes	45%			
Cost of capital	7.0%			
Net cash flow before taxes	(480,120)	606,692	786,692	869,492
Net cash flow after taxes	(264,066)	333,681	432,681	478,221
Annual ROI: direct & indirect benefits				**157%**
Annual ROI: direct benefits only				123%
Net Present Value (NPV)				816,076
Payback period				**0.8 years**
Average Annual Cost of Ownership				368,192
3-Year IRR				131%

All calculations are based on Nucleus Research's independent analysis of the expected costs and benefits associated with the solution.

SALESFORCE COMMERCECLOUD
FOOD PRODUCER

THE BOTTOM LINE

A specialty foods producer deployed Demandware (since acquired by Salesforce and renamed Commerce Cloud) to enable future growth, leverage new technologies, and overhaul its e-commerce arm. Moving away from an aging on-premise application allowed the company to modernize its e-commerce presence so it could leverage new and existing technologies and enable growth in a highly competitive market. Notable benefits achieved include increased developer productivity and increased conversion rates from improved mobile, tablet, and desktop usability.

- ROI: 66%
- Payback: 1.8 Years

THE COMPANY

The company profiled in the case study is a specialty foods producer and retailer based in the Northeastern US. What started as a family-run operation now does business online worldwide and hosts over 500,000 visitors to the headquarters and attached store each year.

THE CHALLENGE

Before the deployment, the company was using an on-premise version of E1 Commerce. The system was inflexible and cumbersome to configure; code updates were scheduled and batched, and the system didn't support a mobile Web site which was a major handicap to growth in the Web-based economy. These factors, plus a lack of available third-party integrations, and an unclear future upgrade path made it an easy decision to transition to a more modern e-commerce solution.

In its new e-commerce system, it knew it needed a cloud-based solution with the following characteristics:

- Usable across multiple device forms.
- Easily configurable to enable rapid changes to the Web site.
- Built-in artificial intelligence (AI) to leverage e-commerce data to derive analytic insights in real-time.
- Able to innovate and compete on the system with regular updates and integration with common third-party vendors.

THE STRATEGY

In 2014 the company began exploring different options, considering Salesforce Commerce Cloud (then Demandware), MarketLive, Magento, or upgrading its legacy system. After a series of meetings with local Demandware reps, the company was confident that a solution to meet its needs could be configured, and in 2015 the project began. Ultimately, Commerce Cloud was chosen for the following key reasons:

- **Cloud-based.** With Commerce Cloud, users can access the system on any connected device, which enables remote access to the site and ensures that company data is up-to-date.
- **Predictive analytics.** The company needed a solution that supported predictive analytics to facilitate intelligent search and product recommendations on its revamped Web site.
- **Backend integrations.** The company needed an e-commerce solution that could easily integrate with its enterprise resource planning (ERP) software, Microsoft Dynamics NAV.

The project team was made up of 12 people who dedicated between 25 and 50 percent of their time to supporting the deployment. The team worked with Pixel Media to implement the system with October 2015 set as the target launch date. A platform transition is a highly involved undertaking, so as the project progressed, the company decided to delay the launch until 2016, and instead use the final quarter of 2015 to address any development snags and to maximize revenue generation in the key holiday season. The system officially went live in March 2016 (after being online for six months Salesforce acquired Demandware and the solution officially became Commerce Cloud).

After Salesforce acquired Demandware in 2016, the company chose to remain with Commerce Cloud because it liked the direction Salesforce was taking, including features such as Einstein, and the increased level of customer support; it was optimistic that Salesforce would continue to invest in Commerce Cloud.

To train users on the system, the company held an on-site bootcamp. Eight users in the pilot program received six hours of training. Post-launch, three additional users were given 10 hours of instruction to onboard them to the system.

KEY BENEFIT AREAS

Deploying Commerce Cloud to modernize its e-commerce capabilities enabled the company to optimize the effectiveness of its Web site, eliminate legacy technology costs, and improve staff productivity. Key benefits of the project included:

- **Increased profits.** Predictive analytics power the product recommendation engine for shoppers on the Web site, enabling intelligent search and presenting similar products to the user within their cart for cross-selling. Eighteen percent of the company's revenues are attributed to e-commerce with 10-15 percent of those sales coming from product suggestions driven by Einstein on the new site. Users are spending more time on the new site with abandonment down 10 percent since deployment. Lead conversion has also increased as a result of the project; on mobile devices it's up 45 percent, for tablets it has increased by 20 percent, while on desktop it's up 10 to 15 percent.
- **Eliminated Rackspace support.** With the legacy solution, the company used Rackspace for hosting and to deliver feedback to improve the stability of its Web site. Using Commerce Cloud, it hasn't needed

dedicated IT support at that scale and realized cost savings by eliminating the Rackspace subscription.
- **Better visibility for decision making.** The deployment granted operators at the company increased operational visibility into sales processes and customer experience. To achieve a comparable level on the legacy system, it would have needed to hire additional staff.
- **Increased productivity.** With Commerce Cloud, team leaders have improved operational visibility which they can use to more efficiently delegate tasks internally. Since the launch, the company has been able to redeploy 25 percent of 3 users' time toward high-value tasks.

KEY COST AREAS

The largest cost area of the company's deployment was implementation consulting from Pixel, followed by the Commerce Cloud subscription costs. Other cost areas over the 3-year period included ongoing consulting, initial and ongoing personnel time to support the project, and user training.

LESSONS LEARNED

This deployment highlights the potential benefits of transitioning from an on-premise to a cloud-based software solution. Despite initial security concerns, software-as-a-service (SaaS) delivers improved user accessibility to the system and easier compatibility with mobile devices, which befits a modern retailer participating in e-commerce. With this project, when it became clear that it wouldn't be ready to go live late in 2015, it was important to delay the timeline and ensure the transition was not rushed and that each feature was properly tested prior to the release. As the fourth quarter of the year is historically peak retail season, it was imperative that the company didn't disrupt its sales potential with an incomplete deployment.

Additionally, the project demonstrates how in an increasingly competitive retail space, vendors need to differentiate on experience, not just product, in order to maximize earnings. As more and more customers are making purchases with mobile devices, to remain viable the company needed to enable mobile shopping.

CALCULATING THE ROI

Nucleus Research analyzed the costs of software, hardware, personnel, consulting, and training over a 3-year period to quantify the company's investment in Salesforce technology. Direct and indirect benefits were also quantified over the 3-year period.

Direct benefits quantified included the elimination of Rackspace support costs, cost savings from a redeployed staff member, and increased profits from improvements to the Web site.

Indirect benefits quantified included increased user productivity. We calculated the indirect benefits using the fully loaded cost per hour of employees. Time savings were multiplied by a correction factor to account for the inefficient transfer of time between time saved and additional time worked.

Not quantified were the additional revenues generated by the implementation of Einstein recommendations on the revamped Website.

Financial Analysis

Annual ROI: 66% • Payback Period: 1.8 years

Benefits	Pre-Start	Year 1	Year 2	Year 3
Direct	0	867,500	867,500	867,500
Indirect	0	50,625	50,625	50,625
Total per period	**0**	**918,125**	**918,125**	**918,125**

Costs—Capitalized Assets	Pre-Start	Year 1	Year 2	Year 3
Software	0	0	0	0
Hardware	0	0	0	0
Project consulting & personnel	0	60,000	0	0
Total per period	**0**	**60,000**	**0**	**0**

Costs—Depreciation	Pre-Start	Year 1	Year 2	Year 3
Software	0	0	0	0
Hardware	0	0	0	0
Project consulting & personnel	0	0	12,000	12,000
Total per period	**0**	**0**	**12,000**	**12,000**

Costs—Depreciation	Pre-Start	Year 1	Year 2	Year 3
Software	230,000	230,000	230,000	0
Hardware	0	0	0	0
Consulting	600,000	42,000	42,000	42,000
Personnel	135,000	50,625	50,625	50,625
Training	2,531	0	0	0
Other	0	0	0	0
Total per period	**967,531**	**322,625**	**322,625**	**92,625**

Financial Analysis	Results	Year 1	Year 2	Year 3
All government taxes	45%			
Cost of capital	7.0%			
Net cash flow before taxes	(967,531)	535,500	595,500	825,500
Net cash flow after taxes	(532,142)	267,525	332,925	459,425
Annual ROI: direct & indirect benefits				**66%**
Annual ROI: direct benefits only				61%
Net Present Value (NPV)				383,698
Payback period				**1.8 years**
Average Annual Cost of Ownership				588,469
3-Year IRR				39%

All calculations are based on Nucleus Research's independent analysis of the expected costs and benefits associated with the solution.

SALESFORCE
BCBS MICHIGAN

THE BOTTOM LINE

Blue Cross Blue Shield of Michigan deployed Salesforce Marketing Cloud, Service Cloud, and Community Cloud to streamline and automate its engagement with members. Nucleus found that the project increased efficiency, accelerated the time to execute mail campaigns by 88 percent, saved $5 million per year in outside agency fees, and brought all their data into a single platform for more effective decision making.

- ROI: 137%
- Payback: 10 Months

THE COMPANY

Blue Cross Blue Shield of Michigan (BCBSM) is a nonprofit mutual insurance corporation founded in 1939. Working as the chief healthcare insurer in Michigan, it runs a large network of hospitals and doctors: 152 hospitals and more than 33,000 doctors. With more than 8,100 employees, Blue Cross provides 6.1 million people with health benefit plans including Employer, Individual, Medicare, Medicaid, dental and vision, and traditional wellness. Headquartered in Detroit, BCBSM has walk-in locations statewide.

THE CHALLENGE

BCBSM had grown its agent network using a combination of custom tools and applications, and with 2500 active agents managed by an external service, it had traditionally focused at a high-level instead of agents' and employees' interactions with individual members. This presented a number of challenges in a competitive environment:

Because of maturing tools and multiple applications, it took more than 60 days to execute on marketing and communications campaigns to members.

With 9 different systems and applications, agents were challenged to find the latest information on members and were unable to drill down to specific vendor records and weren't easily able to identify opportunities for resale and upsell. Adding to this challenge, an external agency that acted on behalf of BCBSM cost approximately $5 million in fees annually.

Internally, BCBSM had a lack of visibility into interactions between members, agents, and employees, which hindered its ability to make data-driven decisions about the business.

Given these challenges, BCBSM looked at a new technology strategy with the goal of increasing operational efficiency and data-driven decision making.

THE STRATEGY

The company considered a number of different technology options and ultimately chose Salesforce for three main reasons: Salesforce' existing investment in capabilities that support insurers; the ability of Salesforce to meet BCBSM's needs across sales, marketing, and service with one solution; and the broader capabilities of Salesforce ecosystem partners. The decision was made in January 2016. The internal core team of six people managed the implementation, working with Accenture over a 10-month period to configure and implement Marketing Cloud, MyBlue Agent Community (based on Community Cloud), and Service Cloud.

Given the scale of the transformation and the number of agents and employees that would be adopting the solution, BCBSM made a significant investment in communicating about the transition and promoting the benefits to end users. The team used a combination of newsletters, FAQs, demos of upcoming features, and in-person training. Initially, they had planned a pilot to a small group of users, but ultimately decided to release it to all users at once to avoid duplicate systems. The internal Salesforce team participated in significant training as well, both in classroom and through Trailhead, obtaining 1,446 badges.

KEY BENEFIT AREAS

Deploying Salesforce enabled BCBSM to increase operational efficiency and data driven decision making while ultimately improving both agent and member engagement. Key benefits of the project included:

- **Greater visibility.** Implementing Salesforce improved agents' ability to access member information and allowed BCBSM insight on agent and employee activity.
- **Improved technology management.** Moving to Salesforce supported a broader reorganization of IT to streamline its operations, enabling the company to increase IT staff productivity, eliminate the cost and labor associated with supporting legacy systems, and move to an agile development model to more effectively meet the ongoing needs of the business.
- **Reduced printing and mailing costs.** Salesforce Marketing Cloud reduced direct mailing time by 88 percent and reduced time and resources by 25 percent.
- **Reduced outside agency fees.** Elimination of a third-party agency to support agents allowed BCBSM to reduce costs by $5 million a year.
- Increased productivity. The MyBlue agent community consolidated member information giving easy access to agents and automated applications, Welcome Journey, mailings, and notices.

KEY COST AREAS

Costs of the project included software subscription fees, initial and ongoing personnel to support the application, staff training time and costs, consulting fees, and the cost of Dreamforce travel.

LESSONS LEARNED

As with any digital transformation of this scale, change management is a key factor in successful adoption. BCBSM recognized this and, early on in the deployment, began promoting the capabilities of the new solution as a tool to enable agents and employees to be more productive and find information with less frustration. The team invested in marketing the benefits of the solution for the individual user more than the functions and features themselves, to drive effective adoption.

CALCULATING THE ROI

Nucleus quantified the costs of the software subscription, third-party consulting, personnel time, and employee training and time that BCBSM incurred over the three-year period in its Salesforce initiative.

Direct benefits quantified included elimination of third-party agency fees, redeployed IT staff, eliminated legacy system support costs, and reduced printing and mailing costs.

Indirect benefits quantified reduced time and resources spent on marketing.

Salesforce: BCBS Michigan

Financial Analysis

Annual ROI: 66% • Payback Period: 1.8 years

Benefits	Pre-Start	Year 1	Year 2	Year 3
Direct	0	7,917,920	7,917,920	7,917,920
Indirect	0	2,500,000	2,500,000	2,500,000
Total per period	**0**	**10,417,920**	**10,417,920**	**10,417,920**

Costs—Capitalized Assets	Pre-Start	Year 1	Year 2	Year 3
Software	0	0	0	0
Hardware	0	0	0	0
Project consulting & personnel	0	0	0	0
Total per period	**0**	**0**	**0**	**0**

Costs—Depreciation	Pre-Start	Year 1	Year 2	Year 3
Software	0	0	0	0
Hardware	0	0	0	0
Project consulting & personnel	0	0	0	0
Total per period	**0**	**0**	**0**	**0**

Costs—Depreciation	Pre-Start	Year 1	Year 2	Year 3
Software	825,000	1,100,000	1,100,000	0
Hardware	0	0	0	0
Consulting	2,900,000	992,000	0	0
Personnel	1,200,000	2,000,000	2,000,000	2,000,000
Training	397,500	0	0	0
Other	0	48,350	48,350	48,350
Total per period	**5,322,500**	**4,140,350**	**3,148,350**	**2,048,350**

Financial Analysis	Results	Year 1	Year 2	Year 3
All government taxes	45%			
Cost of capital	7.0%			
Net cash flow before taxes	(5,322,500)	6,277,570	7,269,570	8,369,570
Net cash flow after taxes	(2,927,375)	3,452,663	3,998,263	4,603,263
Annual ROI: direct & indirect benefits				137%
Annual ROI: direct benefits only				90%
Net Present Value (NPV)				7,549,286
Payback period				**0.8 years**
Average Annual Cost of Ownership				4,886,517
3-Year IRR				115%

All calculations are based on Nucleus Research's independent analysis of the expected costs and benefits associated with the solution.

SALESFORCE
PADUCAH BANK

THE BOTTOM LINE

Paducah Bank deployed Salesforce Financial Services Cloud to standardize its sales process, centralize company information, and provide a unified view of the customer across all business arms, both commercial and retail. Because of the deployment, it was able to avoid custom configuration costs on the legacy system, increase productivity across management and sales, and avoid the cost of an additional hire.

- ROI: 52%
- Payback: 2.3 Years

THE COMPANY

Paducah Bank (PB) is an employee-owned bank headquartered in Paducah, Kentucky. It manages six branch locations around the Paducah and Louisville areas, and employs 150 people. Paducah Bank is a full-service bank, offering both commercial and retail services to its customers. Recent filings state that it manages approximately $650 million in assets.

THE CHALLENGE

Internally, a lack of cross-departmental visibility necessitated regular costly meetings to ensure transparency throughout the organization. Over the last 10 years, physical branch traffic has decreased by 50 percent, and PB realized that the same customer service-based strategy that had been an effective differentiator in the past was no longer sufficient to fuel continued growth in the modern marketplace. There were no standardized sales or reporting processes, and users were logging activity in whatever tool they chose—Excel, Outlook, or pen-paper, to name a few. As a result, there was no visibility into the day-to-day interactions with individual customers. To progress, PB needed to invest in an IT strategy that treated data as an asset to be leveraged instead of a static expense to be managed.

THE STRATEGY

An executive committee was responsible for selecting a vendor and managing the implementation. Many at the company had poor prior experiences with customer relationship management (CRM) technologies and saw them as punitive tools for micromanagement, so the first step in the project was demonstrating the value to prospective users. A representative from Salesforce came to the office for a meeting, and it became evident that both company cultures aligned with the belief that technology should be used to augment customer relationships instead of to replace them. PB also considered Microsoft Dynamics 365 and a custom-built CRM solution but chose Salesforce Financial Services Cloud for the following reasons:

- **Data management.** PB needed a platform that unified company data across business arms in one centralized data hub. It needed to be able to efficiently store, process, analyze, and govern its data to facilitate cross-departmental collaboration and visibility.
- **Ease of use and customization.** The platform needed to be highly usable to spur adoption; to accommodate the dynamic nature of financial services, PB required a solution that allowed the creation of custom objects and fields.
- **Community support.** PB knew that with Salesforce it gained membership to a global community of users in the financial services sector.

The committee was formed in mid-2016; PB signed a contract with Salesforce in December 2017 and the deployment began in February 2018.

Silverline was brought in as an implementation partner and to train the initial users. 25 users received 1-2 hours total of weekly demos and training from Silverline, with additional one-on-one classroom training from internal administrators. Trailheads, the user training framework by Salesforce is just beginning to be used to onboard new users.

KEY BENEFIT AREAS

Deploying the Financial Services Cloud allowed Paducah Bank to improve cross-departmental visibility and cooperation, standardize the sales process, and capitalize operational and customer data to drive growth. Key benefits of the project included the following:

- **Avoided consulting costs.** On the legacy data management provider, to add additional fields to a customer profile would have required extensive developer configuration at additional cost. With Salesforce, users can easily update the profile and begin collecting client information overnight with no extra spending.
- **Avoided hiring additional staff.** On the legacy system, there was one full time administrator whose sole-responsibility was data entry and static reporting. This worker retired prior to the deployment and Paducah Bank was able to avoid a replacement hire due to the ease of data management with Salesforce.
- **Increased productivity.** Users and managers both save one hour per week as a result of the deployment, primarily from less time spent searching for data as it is now all centralized on the Financial Services Cloud.

KEY COST AREAS

The largest cost areas of the deployment were the Salesforce software subscriptions and the third-party consulting services from Silverline. Other costs over the three-year period included initial and ongoing personnel costs to implement and support the solution, as well as the cost of employee time spent training on the new system.

LESSONS LEARNED

Prior to configuring the Financial Services Cloud according to the PB sales pipeline, a standardized sales process needed to be defined. On the legacy system, each user managed their own pipeline using their own preferred tools and methods. Using the deployment as an impetus to standardize, PB defined its processes and created records and workflows to suit them. An interested observer could learn from this deployment to clearly outline and standardize the processes that are going to be supported on-platform prior to beginning the deployment. This would decrease the time from project start to go-live, and reduce the total implementation costs, resulting in a higher ROI.

CALCULATING THE ROI

Nucleus Research analyzed the costs of software, hardware, personnel, consulting, and training over a three-year period to quantify Paducah Bank's investment in Salesforce technology. Direct and indirect benefits were also quantified over a three-year period.

Direct benefits quantified included the avoided costs of consulting needed to implement custom additions to the legacy system, and the savings from avoiding the hire of one data administrator.

Indirect benefits quantified included user and manager productivity. We calculated the indirect benefits from increased productivity using the fully loaded cost per hour of the employees. Time savings were multiplied by a correction factor to account for the inefficient transfer of time.

Salesforce: Paducah Bank

Financial Analysis

Annual ROI: 52% • Payback Period: 2.3 years

Benefits	Pre-Start	Year 1	Year 2	Year 3
Direct	0	301,250	301,250	301,250
Indirect	0	60,750	60,750	60,750
Total per period	**0**	**362,000**	**362,000**	**362,000**

Costs—Capitalized Assets	Pre-Start	Year 1	Year 2	Year 3
Software	0	0	0	0
Hardware	0	0	0	0
Project consulting & personnel	0	0	0	0
Total per period	**0**	**0**	**0**	**0**

Costs—Depreciation	Pre-Start	Year 1	Year 2	Year 3
Software	0	0	0	0
Hardware	0	0	0	0
Project consulting & personnel	0	0	0	0
Total per period	**0**	**0**	**0**	**0**

Costs—Depreciation	Pre-Start	Year 1	Year 2	Year 3
Software	168,500	168,500	168,500	0
Hardware	0	0	0	0
Consulting	95,000	0	0	0
Personnel	63,909	72,900	72,900	72,900
Training	14,202	0	0	0
Other	0	0	0	0
Total per period	**341,611**	**241,400**	**241,400**	**72,900**

Financial Analysis	Results	Year 1	Year 2	Year 3
All government taxes	45%			
Cost of capital	7.0%			
Net cash flow before taxes	(341,611)	120,600	120,600	289,100
Net cash flow after taxes	(187,886)	66,330	66,330	159,005
Annual ROI: direct & indirect benefits				**52%**
Annual ROI: direct benefits only				34%
Net Present Value (NPV)				61,835
Payback period				**2.3 years**
Average Annual Cost of Ownership				299,104
3-Year IRR				22%

All calculations are based on Nucleus Research's independent analysis of the expected costs and benefits associated with the solution.

SALESFORCE LIGHTNING
INSURANCE COMPANY

THE BOTTOM LINE

The company deployed Salesforce Lightning to upgrade the functionality of its existing Sales Cloud deployment. It used Lightning to enable faster data exploration and automated repeated processes across the complete sales cycle to enable more efficient and optimized sales operations. The primary benefits achieved as a result of the deployment included an increase in general user productivity facilitated by more streamlined data search, and an additional increase in administrator productivity from completing reports 25 percent faster which saved admins an average of 3 hours per week.

- ROI: 500%
- Payback: 2.4 Months

THE COMPANY

The company is a global provider of financial risk management products and services, specializing in warranty solutions and benefits. It operates in over 35 countries worldwide and employs a workforce of over 1500 people. It serves enterprise customers, primarily in the retail space, as well as financial institutions.

THE CHALLENGE

Sales Cloud was deployed in 2005 to meet basic customer relationship management (CRM) needs but was only used for basic pipeline management and didn't achieve widespread adoption. In 2014 the company began internal discussions to relaunch the platform more effectively. Administrators met with department leaders to outline business processes and how they could be improved with on the system. As the project team learned more about available Salesforce products that could add value to the business, a migration to Salesforce Lightning stood out for its ease-of-use and how it could dramatically expedite sales processes to boost agent productivity.

THE STRATEGY

To explore the feasibility of a Lightning migration for the company, an administrator completed the Lightning readiness assessment with assistance from a Salesforce Lightning implementation expert. Although the company had created many customized records and fields within Sales Cloud, it hadn't configured many custom processes requiring backend integrations, so the report indicated that it would be an easy upgrade to migrate to Lightning.

A month-long pilot for 25 users was launched in March 2018, with each user being given 8-10 assignments on Lightning weekly to gain familiarity and build confidence using the system. The month of April was spent incorporating and testing suggestions for improvements from pilot-users. In May, the official training program and rollout commenced for all US-based staff, and their improvement suggestions were built-on in June. The end of July signaled the completion of the global rollout for users worldwide with 473 people currently online using the platform. All users received 1.5 hours of training via a live webinar.

The project was completed internally without any third-party consulting, and took 80 hours of administrator time, with 8 additional business people with Salesforce training providing approximately 30 percent of their time to support the deployment for one month. The most labor-intensive aspect of the transition was configuring the page layouts for custom objects in Lightning and meeting with the users to ensure that the converted objects functioned correctly.

Currently, all users are live using Lightning and the configuration team is looking out for recommendations from non-US users to improve the platform. Users have all been taught how to use Lightning and how to convert back to Sales Cloud Classic if they need to, and managers are working to create dashboards that track internal adoption.

KEY BENEFIT AREAS

The main benefit realized because of the Lightning adoption was increased productivity for users and administrators alike. With task automation and custom processes built in Lightning, users found themselves spending less time on repeatable tasks, like data entry and data quality verification, and were able to dedicate more effort to serving customers.

- **Increased user productivity.** Lightning streamlines the process to create and edit records and facilitates global search of data on the platform. With Favorites, users get easy access to the files they most commonly use. Users spend less time searching for the data they need to use, with each of the 473 users saving an average of 30 minutes per week.
- **Increased administrator productivity.** With Lightning the data is stored in a more organized framework on the backend, so validation processes can be run more smoothly. The added structure expedites report-generation, allowing the three internal admins to complete reporting tasks in 25 percent of the time it took on Classic and save approximately 3 hours per week.

KEY COST AREAS

Since the implementation was executed internally, the largest cost area for the deployment was employee time spent in training as all 473 users received 1.5 hours of instruction to become proficient with the system. The only other cost was the personnel time for the implementation team, composed of one administrator and 8 other employees. No third-party consultants were used, and there were no additional software or hardware expenses incurred during the upgrade as Lightning is included with Sales Cloud.

LESSONS LEARNED

Completing the Lightning Readiness Report prior to beginning the deployment was a key step that indicated the feasibility and value of the project. In this case, the results indicated that the company was a good fit and could transition to Lightning without a complex or expensive integration process. Because of this, the company did not hire third-party consultants to assist with the project, and instead kept the team in-house, which lowered implementation costs.

The high readiness score was produced because the company's Sales Cloud deployment was simple without a lot of custom integrations or backend configuration. It did, however, have a large portfolio of custom objects that were in use on the platform, and the most time-consuming aspect of the deployment was ensuring that these custom-built objects functioned as-intended in Lightning. For deployments entailing less custom configuration, an even shorter project duration would be expected.

CALCULATING THE ROI

Nucleus Research analyzed the costs of software, hardware, personnel, consulting, and training over a 3-year period to quantify the company's investment in Salesforce technology. Direct and indirect benefits were also quantified over the 3-year period.

There were no direct benefits identified as a result of the deployment.

Indirect benefits quantified included increases in productivity to both users and administrators. We calculated the productivity benefits using the fully loaded cost per hour of employees. Time savings were then multiplied by a correction factor to account for the inefficient transfer of time between time saved and additional time worked.

Salesforce Lightning: Insurance Company

Financial Analysis

Annual ROI: 500% • Payback Period: 0.2 years

Benefits	Pre-Start	Year 1	Year 2	Year 3
Direct	0	0	0	0
Indirect	0	246,975	246,975	246,975
Total per period	**0**	**246,975**	**246,975**	**246,975**

Costs—Capitalized Assets	Pre-Start	Year 1	Year 2	Year 3
Software	0	0	0	0
Hardware	0	0	0	0
Project consulting & personnel	0	0	0	0
Total per period	**0**	**0**	**0**	**0**

Costs—Depreciation	Pre-Start	Year 1	Year 2	Year 3
Software	0	0	0	0
Hardware	0	0	0	0
Project consulting & personnel	0	0	0	0
Total per period	**0**	**0**	**0**	**0**

Costs—Depreciation	Pre-Start	Year 1	Year 2	Year 3
Software	0	0	0	0
Hardware	0	0	0	0
Consulting	0	0	0	0
Personnel	20,894	0	0	0
Training	28,551	0	0	0
Other	0	0	0	0
Total per period	**49,444**	**0**	**0**	**0**

Financial Analysis	Results	Year 1	Year 2	Year 3
All government taxes	45%			
Cost of capital	7.0%			
Net cash flow before taxes	(49,444)	246,975	246,975	246,975
Net cash flow after taxes	(27,194)	135,836	135,836	135,836
Annual ROI: direct & indirect benefits				**500%**
Annual ROI: direct benefits only				0%
Net Present Value (NPV)				329,283
Payback period				**0.2 years**
Average Annual Cost of Ownership				16,481
3-Year IRR				497%

All calculations are based on Nucleus Research's independent analysis of the expected costs and benefits associated with the solution.

SALESFORCE LIGHTNING
ASPECT

THE BOTTOM LINE

Aspect upgraded its Salesforce Sales Cloud to Lightning to modernize its user experience and drive greater adoption. Nucleus found that the project enabled the company to increase sales, reduce user help-desk demands, and increase visibility across the organization to improve customer engagement.

- ROI: 636%
- Payback: 2 months
- Average annual benefit: $2,095,550

THE COMPANY

Aspect was founded in 1973 when it built the first call center flight booking system with automatic call distribution for Continental Airlines. Since then, the company has grown to be a global leader in contact center applications, serving customers in 115 countries. Based in Phoenix, Arizona, the company has approximately 300 sales people.

THE CHALLENGE

Given the nature of Aspect's business, it had a very complex product set with a matrix pricing model that was required to develop quotes for customers. The company had been a Salesforce Sales Cloud and Service Cloud customer for some time, but quoting was handled through the company's Oracle E-Business Suite enterprise resource planning (ERP) application and involved a number of manual workarounds: quotes would be developed on Excel spreadsheets, circulated via e-mail, and then manually uploaded into the E-Business Suite quoting system.

As part of a broader sales and technology strategy initiative in 2015, the company replaced Oracle with NetSuite, a redesigned Salesforce Sales Cloud, and a quoting engine provided by a Salesforce ecosystem partner. However, because of Aspect's complex product set and pricing model, the quoting component still required the completion of a number of custom fields. This posed problems including:

- Performance issues. The number of custom fields and frequency of their use was slowing application performance as the highly-customized application met Salesforce limits.
- Despite the customizations, sales people still had to complete a number of manual steps to enter their quotes. This was not only creating an undue burden on sales people: it was also driving a significant volume of help-desk tickets as users needed support to complete the quoting process.

THE STRATEGY

Aspect decided to implement a new sales methodology (customer-centric selling) in 2015. After seeing Lightning at Dreamforce, the company developed a plan to implement Lightning Experience, Salesforce's new Lightning user interface (UI), with the next phase of its sales methodology. Beginning in mid-2016, Aspect's Salesforce technology leadership began meeting with the sales operations team to determine how Lightning Experience could be used to support customer-centric selling.

Because Aspect had a strong internal Salesforce team, it didn't need to bring in outside consultants, and the actual deployment including the built-in sales methodology, automated activity updating, and guided selling was completed by a team of three Salesforce leads and 15 business users (on a part-time basis) in three months.

Aspect devoted approximately three hours of demos and informal training on the new UI and sales methodology at its 2016 sales kickoff, and a new Lightning-based partner product configuration engine was rolled out 9 months later.

Today, sales people are taking advantage of the automated quoting process and updated information is available to both the management team and the customer service and contract renewals teams, who now know that they have up-to-date and accurate quote information within the system.

KEY BENEFIT AREAS

Moving to Lightning has enabled Aspect to drive greater visibility and productivity across its organization, from sales to management to customer support. Key benefits of the project include:

- **Improved reporting and visibility.** Prior to Lightning, Aspect had one full-time business analyst devoted to gathering, scrubbing, and reporting on sales pipeline data. Additionally, there was significant volatility in the pipeline as pipeline reporting was somewhat manual and subjective. Today, much of that process has been standardized and automated, and the entire management team reviews sales progress and bookings directly in a Salesforce Lightning dashboard. The analyst previously tasked with pipeline reporting has been promoted to other activities.
- **Increased profits.** The combination of customer-centric selling and the guided "Sales Path" capabilities of Lightning Experience — as well as its intuitive UI — has increased sales productivity and the ability to focus on deals most likely to close, enabling Aspect to increase its close rates by 25 percent.
- **Improved renewal operations.** Nearly half of Aspect's annual revenues comes from renewals, and the renewals team now has up-to-date and accurate account details for each customer. An automated quote generation process that is launched one year from the initial contract closing date has increased productivity for the team by 15 percent, because they no no longer have to manually review and validate account information before beginning the renewal process.
- **Increased IT support staff productivity.** Aspect has been able to reduce the overall volume of help desk tickets associated with Sales Cloud. It has also reduced the mean active time to resolution for cases by 83 percent, freeing up time for other activities.

KEY COST AREAS

Key cost areas for the project included software license subscription fees, personnel time to implement the project, and the cost of sales people's time spent in training. Although Aspect invested in some Salesforce licenses to provide additional users with access to the application, there was no additional fee to upgrade existing Salesforce users to Lightning because Aspect was already a Performance Edition customer.

BEST PRACTICES

Moving to Lightning enabled Aspect to dramatically increase the performance of Sales Cloud while supporting the quoting complexity demanded by its product set. Because Lightning Experience brings a new way to render pages on the Salesforce platform, a modern UI, and guided selling, users now see Sales Cloud as a tool to support them, rather than a hindrance.

Aspect also embedded IT with sales operations through the planning and deployment process to ensure that the ultimate application that was delivered would be perceived as an enabler to sales.

CALCULATING THE ROI

Nucleus quantified the initial and ongoing costs of software license subscription fees, personnel, and training over three years to calculate Aspect's total project investment. As the company already had Sales Cloud and Service Cloud licenses, only the incremental additional investment in subscriptions to provide additional users with access was included in the cost calculations. Because Aspect already had a Salesforce support team in place, there were no additional personnel needed to support the redeployment on an ongoing basis.

The direct benefit quantified included the redeployment of a business analyst and was calculated based on the annual fully loaded cost of that employee. Indirect benefits quantified included the increase in profits attributed to guided selling and the increased productivity of the IT support and renewals team, calculated based on their average annual fully loaded cost using a correction factor to account for the inefficient transfer of time between time saved and additional time worked. Not included in the benefits calculation were the impacts of greater visibility and lower pipeline volatility driven by the project.

Financial Analysis

Annual ROI: 942% • Payback Period: 0.1 years

Benefits	Pre-Start	Year 1	Year 2	Year 3
Direct	0	72,800	72,800	72,800
Indirect	0	2,022,750	2,022,750	2,022,750
Total per period	**0**	**2,095,550**	**2,095,550**	**2,095,550**

Costs—Capitalized Assets	Pre-Start	Year 1	Year 2	Year 3
Software	0	0	0	0
Hardware	0	0	0	0
Project consulting & personnel	0	0	0	0
Total per period	**0**	**0**	**0**	**0**

Costs—Depreciation	Pre-Start	Year 1	Year 2	Year 3
Software	0	0	0	0
Hardware	0	0	0	0
Project consulting & personnel	0	0	0	0
Total per period	**0**	**0**	**0**	**0**

Costs—Depreciation	Pre-Start	Year 1	Year 2	Year 3
Software	150,000	150,000	150,000	0
Hardware	0	0	0	0
Consulting	0	0	0	0
Personnel	130,650	0	0	0
Training	33,000	0	0	0
Other	0	0	0	0
Total per period	**313,650**	**150,000**	**150,000**	**0**

Financial Analysis	Results	Year 1	Year 2	Year 3
All government taxes	45%			
Cost of capital	7.0%			
Net cash flow before taxes	(313,650)	1,945,550	1,945,550	2,095,550
Net cash flow after taxes	(172,508)	1,070,053	1,070,053	1,152,553
Annual ROI: direct & indirect benefits				636%
Annual ROI: direct benefits only				-9%
Net Present Value (NPV)				2,702,993
Payback period				**0.2 years**
Average Annual Cost of Ownership				204,550
3-Year IRR				619%

All calculations are based on Nucleus Research's independent analysis of the expected costs and benefits associated with the solution.

SALESFORCE
TRILOGY FINANCIAL

THE BOTTOM LINE

Trilogy Financial moved to Salesforce Financial Services Cloud to drive a centralized, consistent approach to all its client intake, marketing, sales, and support processes. Nucleus found that the project enabled the company to increase productivity, data accuracy, and visibility across the organization while reducing costs. Prebuilt industry-specific capabilities enabled Trilogy to avoid additional customization and integration work, as well as ongoing administrator support, that would have been needed without Financial Services Cloud.

- ROI: 147%
- Payback: 1 year
- Average annual benefit: $972,091

THE COMPANY

Trilogy Financial is a privately-held financial planning firm with more than $2 billion in client assets. Headquartered in Huntington Beach, CA with 11 offices in the United States, Trilogy Financial's service model focuses on the health and success of Trilogy's team of independent advisors and their ability to support and empower the health and success of their clients.

THE CHALLENGE

Trilogy was founded in the late 1990s with a focus on ensuring client success with a network of independent advisors. As the company expanded, it outgrew its branch-based client database and built a centralized database where all client data was stored. However, as is the case with many networks of advisors, the Trilogy model depended on their advisors to continuously update client data. Although administrative staff was effective at keeping records in areas like correspondence up to date, advisors had varying levels of adoption of the application and, as a result, much of the critical client data didn't make it beyond their personal client databases. As the company positioned for its next level of growth with new products and more stringent compliance requirements, it recognized the need for an enterprise solution that could be easily adopted by independent advisors around the country, as well as one that could be updated and managed on a centralized basis.

THE STRATEGY

The team at Trilogy began exploring new solutions and found that Orion, an account reporting and asset management application the company already used, had a Salesforce integration. At the same time, Salesforce shared its current and future roadmap for Financial Services Cloud with Trilogy. The company decided to move to Financial Services Cloud for three main reasons:

- **Single view of the client.** Financial Services Cloud would give Trilogy one consistent cloud-based platform that could be accessed from anywhere. The platform also easily supported integrations with existing systems as well as new technologies the company planned to adopt, such as marketing automation with Salesforce Pardot.
- **Speed to value.** The investments Salesforce made in the Financial Services Cloud data model would enable Trilogy to capture richer client data—such as householding, financial accounts, and goals—without extensive customization or addition of custom fields. Additionally, Trilogy would be able to automate its client intake process largely with existing functionality built in Financial Services Cloud.
- **Usability.** Trilogy was comfortable that advisors would adopt

Financial Services Cloud and update client data on an ongoing basis as part of their daily work flow, enabling managers to more easily track advisor activity across the business.

The company began deploying Financial Services Cloud in September 2016, using Red Sky Solutions, a Salesforce consulting partner, to support the initial integration and customization work, and went live in January 2017.

The total deployment time was approximately 4 months. Red Sky performed some initial training and the Trilogy internal team delivered both pre-launch and post-launch ongoing training updates. Today, Trilogy is moving beyond initial adoption of advisors, managers, and branch administrators to drive a consistent client experience across all interactions.

KEY BENEFIT AREAS

Moving to one integrated platform has enabled Trilogy to ensure that advisors have all the data and tools they need to provide superior client service while providing managers and administrators with the up-to-date information they need to manage the oversight and compliance requirements of the business. Key benefits of the project include:

- **Increased advisor, manager, administrator, and marketing productivity.** Before Financial Services Cloud, advisors and administrators often had to search for or verify client information to make sure it was correct—and managers were challenged to track progress. Today, all client information is available in one place, and can also be used with confidence by marketing for targeted campaigns.
- **Improved client service.** By automating the client intake process, Trilogy increased data capture and data integrity while ensuring that a complete history of client interactions is available to help advisors give informed and client-specific advice.
- **Improved technology management.** By moving to one integrated platform, Trilogy was able to eliminate costs associated with management of the old system and the workarounds (such as private couriers) that drove additional costs without adding value.

KEY COST AREAS

Key cost areas for the project included software license subscription fees, consulting, personnel time to deploy and support the application, and training time.

BEST PRACTICES

Although Trilogy is still in a relatively early phase of adoption of Financial Services Cloud, it has already seen returns by automating processes—such as client intake—that were previously performed manually. Training on an ongoing basis ensures advisors take full advantage of the application over time as they become more proficient in its use.

Trilogy was initially simply looking for a replacement to its outdated CRM application. However, it found that Financial Services Cloud capabilities including support for householding and client intake, as well as Docusign and Orion integration, enabled it to do more than originally planned: it could automate processes such as client intake with limited customization and integration work.

Nucleus conservatively estimates that, without Financial Services Cloud, Trilogy's costs would have included:

- A 2x investment in initial integration and consulting services to deliver the same capabilities available standard in Financial Services Cloud.
- An additional 25 percent in ongoing Salesforce administrator resources to support customizations and integrations.

CALCULATING THE ROI

Nucleus quantified the initial and ongoing costs of software license subscription fees, consulting, personnel, and training over three years to calculate Trilogy's total investment in Financial Services Cloud.

Direct benefits quantified included the reduction in third-party support costs for the retired custom client database as well as the reduction in courier and document scanning costs driven by the deployment.

Indirect benefits quantified included the increase in financial advisor, manager, and marketing staff productivity driven by the application, and were calculated based on the average annual fully loaded cost of employees in each role, using a correction factor to account for the inefficient transfer of time between time saved and additional time worked. Not quantified was the expected additional business gained by Trilogy that Nucleus expects the company will achieve as it reaches full adoption and can leverage Financial Services Cloud to better market to and service its clients and prospects.

Financial Analysis

Annual ROI: 147% • Payback Period: 1.0 years

Benefits	Pre-Start	Year 1	Year 2	Year 3
Direct	0	110,100	143,400	199,200
Indirect	0	691,609	885,983	885,983
Total per period	**0**	**801,709**	**1,029,383**	**1,085,183**

Costs—Capitalized Assets	Pre-Start	Year 1	Year 2	Year 3
Software	0	0	0	0
Hardware	0	0	0	0
Project consulting & personnel	0	0	0	0
Total per period	**0**	**0**	**0**	**0**

Costs—Depreciation	Pre-Start	Year 1	Year 2	Year 3
Software	0	0	0	0
Hardware	0	0	0	0
Project consulting & personnel	0	0	0	0
Total per period	**0**	**0**	**0**	**0**

Costs—Depreciation	Pre-Start	Year 1	Year 2	Year 3
Software	237,492	263,880	316,656	0
Hardware	0	0	0	0
Consulting	125,000	60,000	60,000	60,000
Personnel	12,500	32,500	65,000	65,000
Training	72,115	9,014	9,014	9,014
Other	0	0	0	0
Total per period	**447,107**	**365,394**	**450,670**	**134,014**

Financial Analysis	Results	Year 1	Year 2	Year 3
All government taxes	45%			
Cost of capital	7.0%			
Net cash flow before taxes	(447,107)	436,315	578,712	951,168
Net cash flow after taxes	(245,909)	239,973	318,292	523,142
Annual ROI: direct & indirect benefits				**147%**
Annual ROI: direct benefits only				-37%
Net Present Value (NPV)				683,413
Payback period				**1.0 years**
Average Annual Cost of Ownership				465,729
3-Year IRR				109%

All calculations are based on Nucleus Research's independent analysis of the expected costs and benefits associated with the solution.

SALESFORCE EINSTEIN ALALYTICS
SHAZAM

THE BOTTOM LINE

Shazam deployed Salesforce Einstein Analytics to provide its employees with a user friendly analytics tool, allowing for ad-hoc analysis. The company had relied on Excel, but found that they were not able to execute on advanced analytics. It needed a solution that would help increase efficiency and reduce requests for reports from the core analytics team. Nucleus found that Salesforce Einstein Analytics helped increase productivity for the chief revenue officer (CRO), the sales VPs, and the analytics team. In addition, the deployment helped Shazam maintain clean data for improved customer segmentation and more effective sales efforts.

- ROI: 752%
- Payback: 1.6 months
- Average annual benefit: $266,873

THE COMPANY

Shazam is one of the most popular apps of all time, used by hundreds of millions of people each month to connect to the world around them. The app has been downloaded over 1 billion times, in over 190 countries, and users Shazam over 20 million times each day.

THE CHALLENGE

Shazam sought to reduce the need for Excel with a solution that would allow for self-service analytics. Previously, any reports or analysis for sales teams were executed by the core analytics team. This was time consuming for the analytics team, and sales VPs were unable to quickly gather up-to-date metrics on the performance of their sales teams.

In addition, the analytics in practice were limited because data was siloed in various spreadsheets, making it difficult and time consuming to clean and consolidate the data for ongoing analysis.

THE STRATEGY

The company discovered Salesforce Einstein Analytics at a Salesforce event, which prompted the team to further explore the possibilities of implementing a new analytics tool. Shazam evaluated other user-friendly analytics applications, but ultimately chose Salesforce Einstein Analytics for a number of reasons including:

- **Usability.** Shazam's user base for Salesforce Einstein Analytics consists primarily of its leadership team. The company understood the critical need to increase the productivity of these highly skilled workers so that they would not be bogged down by clunky applications that are difficult to use on a daily basis.
- **Out-of-the-box capabilities.** The Shazam team found that much of the capabilities they would need for their sales users were already available as pre-built charts and dashboards. As a result, this would significantly reduce time spent on implementation and customization.
- **Budget friendly.** The team found that Salesforce Einstein Analytics fit easily into their budget and was a very affordable option.

Shazam started the deployment in July 2016 and was able to go live by January 2017. The team did not need to hire any third party consultants for their implementation and a single Shazam employee led the project. In addition to leading the deployment, he also spent his time cleaning and consolidating all of the pre-existing CRM data. Salesforce Einstein Analytics was rolled out to nine users, who were trained within a few hours by the same Shazam employee that led the implementation. These users included analysts, sales VPs, and the CRO. After Salesforce Einstein Analytics went live, Shazam built out additional dashboards for new use cases.

KEY BENEFIT AREAS

The Salesforce Einstein Analytics deployment drove increased productivity for Shazam's users, while simultaneously providing them with more advanced functionality. As a result, the company experienced benefits including:

- **Increased employee productivity.** The Salesforce Einstein Analytics users have been able to experience increased productivity because the solution is intuitive and offers ad-hoc analysis capabilities with a clean, centralized data repository. As a result, Sales VPs do not have to ask analysts to run reports for them and they are able to quickly find the metrics they need. In addition, the CRO has been able to increase his productivity by 30 minutes per week.
- **Improved data quality.** Prior to Salesforce Einstein Analytics, analytics users spent an average of 15 percent of their time cleaning data because the information had to be collected and analyzed using Excel. Today, this data cleansing period has been eliminated and users can spend more time analyzing instead of spending hours on tedious data cleansing.
- **Improved customer segementation.** With Salesforce Einstein Analytics, Shazam is able to obtain more detailed information on its customers. For example, the company can identify more granular patterns by region, allowing their sales teams to more accurately target their customer base.
- **Improved analyst retention.** Salesforce Einstein Analytics has removed much of the tedious report building from the hands of the analyst team. Therefore, the analysts can spend more time dong advanced analytics that better satisfies their skill set, encouraging them to remain at the company for a longer period of time.

KEY COST AREAS

Costs of the project included software licenses fees, a one-time implementation fee, personnel time to implement and support the application, and user training time.

BEST PRACTICES

Prior to implementing Salesforce Einstein Analytics, Shazam had inconsistencies in approximately half of their account data. This is not uncommon for a CRM system, because it is extremely difficult to maintain consistency when inputting account contact information. For example, one salesperson may enter "Nucleus Research," and another salesperson may enter "Nucleus Research LLC." Neither of these are wrong, but the salespeople have inadvertently created duplicate records for "Nucleus Research."

Before going live with Salesforce Einstein Analytics, the lead on the implementation spent considerable time cleaning the data to remove any duplicates or inaccuracies. In addition, the team set up new guidelines for entering data that has allowed them to maintain an accuracy level of approximately 90 percent. A 90 percent accuracy level for CRM data is strong and has allowed Shazam to more easily use the data for their analyses.

CALCULATING THE ROI

Nucleus quantified the initial and ongoing costs of software license fees, implementation fees, personnel time to implement and support the application, employee training time, and consulting over a 3-year period to calculate Shazam's total investment in Salesforce Einstein Analytics.

Indirect benefits quantified included the increase in productivity for the CRO, sales VPs, and analysts. These productivity savings were quantified based on the average annual fully loaded cost of an employee using a correction factor to account for the inefficient transfer between time saved and additional time worked. Not quantified is the impact on sales that has materialized from a better understanding of their customer base.

Financial Analysis

Annual ROI: 752% • Payback Period: 0.1 years

Benefits	Pre-Start	Year 1	Year 2	Year 3
Direct	0	0	0	0
Indirect	0	266,873	266,873	266,873
Total per period	**0**	**266,873**	**266,873**	**266,873**

Costs—Capitalized Assets	Pre-Start	Year 1	Year 2	Year 3
Software	0	0	0	0
Hardware	0	0	0	0
Project consulting & personnel	0	0	0	0
Total per period	**0**	**0**	**0**	**0**

Costs—Depreciation	Pre-Start	Year 1	Year 2	Year 3
Software	0	0	0	0
Hardware	0	0	0	0
Project consulting & personnel	0	0	0	0
Total per period	**0**	**0**	**0**	**0**

Costs—Depreciation	Pre-Start	Year 1	Year 2	Year 3
Software	6,000	4,500	4,500	0
Hardware	0	0	0	0
Consulting	0	0	0	0
Personnel	28,350	5,452	5,452	5,452
Training	0	227	0	0
Other	0	0	0	0
Total per period	**34,350**	**10,179**	**9,952**	**5,452**

Financial Analysis	Results	Year 1	Year 2	Year 3
All government taxes	45%			
Cost of capital	7.0%			
Net cash flow before taxes	(34,350)	256,694	256,921	261,421
Net cash flow after taxes	(18,893)	141,182	141,307	143,782
Annual ROI: direct & indirect benefits				**752%**
Annual ROI: direct benefits only				-25%
Net Present Value (NPV)				353,845
Payback period				**0.1 years**
Average Annual Cost of Ownership				19,978
3-Year IRR				746%

All calculations are based on Nucleus Research's independent analysis of the expected costs and benefits associated with the solution.

SALESFORCE
RACK ROOM SHOES

THE BOTTOM LINE

Rack Room Shoes and Off Broadway Shoe Warehouse deployed Salesforce Marketing Cloud to expand, customize, and unify their marketing campaigns. The companies leveraged their employees' existing knowledge of Salesforce to move away from a third-party vendor and build an internal marketing team. Nucleus found that the deployment increased revenue and productivity.

- ROI: 777%
- Payback: 2 months
- Average annual benefit: $11,122,990

THE COMPANY

Rack Room Shoes and Off Broadway Shoe Warehouse sell shoes in a variety of styles for men, women, and children online and in brick-and-mortar stores across the United States. Together the brands have a total of 500 locations with the corporate headquarters in Charlotte, North Carolina, though the Deichmann Group of Germany owns both companies.

THE CHALLENGE

Initially, Rack Room Shoes was using a third-party vendor to manage its e-mail marketing through a batch and blast approach. However, Rack Room Shoes had no visibility into the vendor's activity, and found that the batch e-mails not only contained mistakes, but were often delayed and therefore irrelevant. Meanwhile, the vendor was becoming increasingly expensive as Rack Room Shoes grew and maxed out the number of e-mails the vendor could send and the number of campaigns the vendor could manage.

Additionally, Rack Room Shoes and Off Broadway Shoe Warehouse were running separate e-mail and text marketing programs with siloed marketing teams. Rack Room Shoes wanted to integrate both companies' data, campaigns, and personnel with a single solution.

THE STRATEGY

Rack Room Shoes and Off Broadway Shoe Warehouse worked with the Salesforce partner Digital Fusion, who suggested Salesforce Marketing Cloud. Key features of the Salesforce Marketing Cloud are E-Mail Studio, Salesforce's e-mail marketing platform, and Journey Builder, Salesforce's life cycle management feature. The companies selected the solution for the following reasons:

- **Scalability.** Salesforce would enable the companies to send more e-mails, run more campaigns, and customize their communications.
- **Multiple channels.** Salesforce would allow the companies to send text messages and push notifications to their customers.
- **Previous experience.** The director in charge of the deployment and the employees who would be using the tool all had previous Salesforce experience.

The companies started the deployment in July 2015 and went live in October 2015. They purchased an annual licensing fee for Salesforce Marketing Cloud and fees for additional e-mail addresses. Two employees worked full-time and one employee worked part-time to complete the project. This included transferring existing customer data into the Salesforce Marketing Cloud. The companies also engaged two Digital Fusion consultants in the implementation process.

Today, Rack Room Shoes and Off Broadway Shoe Warehouse have replaced the third-party vendor with a consolidated internal marketing team consisting of two analysts, two communications specialists, and one customer relationship management (CRM) manager and one CRM administrator to support the ongoing use of Salesforce Marketing Cloud. Digital Fusion supports the marketing team on an ongoing basis.

KEY BENEFIT AREAS

Salesforce Marketing Cloud enabled Rack Room Shoes and Off Broadway Shoe Warehouse to automate and add text message to each company's campaigns. Key benefits of the project include:

- **Increased incremental revenue from in-store rewards programs.** Rack Room Shoes and Off Broadway Shoe Warehouse incentivized more in-store sales by getting more customers to use their in-store rewards programs. Now, customers can sign up for in-store rewards with a mobile phone numbers instead of an e-mail address. With Salesforce, the companies can see which customers haven't used their reward and use this information to remind customers to redeem it by shopping in-store.
- **Avoided costs and reallocated resources.** In eliminating the third-party vendor and license fees associated with the vendor, the companies also avoided additional professional service fees associated with increasing the volume of the vendor's work. The companies reinvested their resources by hiring an experienced Salesforce CRM administrator in place of an additional analyst.
- **Increased revenue from e-mail and text message.** Where before the vendor only launched one campaign per week, the companies now use Salesforce's automation to launch many different campaigns every day both via e-mail and text message. The companies can also personalize campaign communications by segmenting their customers using Salesforce Audience Builder.
- **Improved marketer productivity.** The integration of data from both Rack Room Shoes and Off Broadway Shoe Warehouse enhances the usefulness the data the analysts use. With this and automation, marketing analysts now do much more in the time they have.

KEY COST AREAS

Costs of the project included software subscription fees, fees for additional e-mail addresses to market to, consulting costs for implementation, ongoing consulting service fees, and personnel time to implement and support the application on an ongoing basis.

BEST PRACTICES

Rack Room Shoes and Off Broadway Shoe Warehouse did not need to invest in any training to deploy Salesforce Marketing Cloud. The employees who use the product taught themselves because they had all worked with Salesforce in the past. When a company is selecting a new marketing solution, it can pay to invest in a vendor with which the company's employees are already familiar.

CALCULATING THE ROI

To calculate the total investment Rack Room Shoes and Off Broadway Shoe Warehouse made in Salesforce Marketing Cloud, Nucleus quantified the initial and ongoing costs of software subscription fees, e-mail address fees, consulting, and personnel time to implement and support the application on an ongoing basis over a 3-year period.

Direct benefits quantified for Rack Room Shoes and Off Broadway Shoe Warehouse included eliminated costs for third-party vendor service and software license fees, as well as avoided costs for additional professional service fees and the cost of one additional analyst on the internal marketing team. The indirect benefits quantified for both companies included greater profits due to increased in-store revenue from the companies' rewards programs and increased revenue from both e-commerce and text messaging marketing campaigns. These benefits were quantified using revenue, profit margin, and a multiplier to attribute increased earnings directly to Salesforce Marketing Cloud.

Financial Analysis

Annual ROI: 777% • Payback Period: 0.1 years

Benefits	Pre-Start	Year 1	Year 2	Year 3
Direct	0	1,986,000	1,986,000	1,986,000
Indirect	0	8,396,723	9,190,323	9,823,923
Total per period	**0**	**10,382,723**	**11,176,323**	**11,809,923**

Costs—Capitalized Assets	Pre-Start	Year 1	Year 2	Year 3
Software	0	0	0	0
Hardware	0	0	0	0
Project consulting & personnel	0	0	0	0
Total per period	**0**	**0**	**0**	**0**

Costs—Depreciation	Pre-Start	Year 1	Year 2	Year 3
Software	0	0	0	0
Hardware	0	0	0	0
Project consulting & personnel	0	0	0	0
Total per period	**0**	**0**	**0**	**0**

Costs—Depreciation	Pre-Start	Year 1	Year 2	Year 3
Software	1,100,000	1,310,000	1,310,000	0
Hardware	0	0	0	0
Consulting	37,500	490,000	490,000	490,000
Personnel	112,000	48,000	48,000	48,000
Training	0	0	0	0
Other	0	0	0	0
Total per period	**1,249,500**	**1,848,000**	**1,848,000**	**538,000**

Financial Analysis	Results	Year 1	Year 2	Year 3
All government taxes	45%			
Cost of capital	7.0%			
Net cash flow before taxes	(1,249,500)	8,534,723	9,328,323	11,271,923
Net cash flow after taxes	(687,225)	4,694,098	5,130,578	6,199,558
Annual ROI: direct & indirect benefits				**777%**
Annual ROI: direct benefits only				46%
Net Present Value (NPV)				13,241,713
Payback period				**0.1 years**
Average Annual Cost of Ownership				1,827,833
3-Year IRR				692%

All calculations are based on Nucleus Research's independent analysis of the expected costs and benefits associated with the solution.

SALESFORCE SERVICE CLOUD
ROSETTA STONE

THE BOTTOM LINE

Rosetta Stone deployed Salesforce Service Cloud to replace an application that limited its ability to scale and grow. Nucleus found that the Service Cloud deployment enabled the company to reduce average call handling time and increase call deflections to self service and chat, thereby increasing productivity for sales and marketing while improving customer satisfaction.

- ROI: 26%
- Payback: 3 years
- Average annual benefit: $949,217

THE COMPANY

Founded in 1992, Rosetta Stone specializes in providing interactive language-learning solutions. The company's products have been used by millions of users in more than 150 countries, by more than 22,000 educational institutions, and 12,000 corporations. Rosetta has more than 1,100 employees and is headquartered in Arlington, Virginia.

THE CHALLENGE

Rosetta Stone previously relied on Parature (now Microsoft Parature) to support its customer service agents. As the company continued to expand is customer base, however, it began to have performance problems and concerns about scalability, as sometimes it could take a few minutes to retrieve a customer record. Upon further analysis, Rosetta Stone felt that Parature's roadmap didn't support its needs for data integration and growth and that it needed to find a new service automation solution.

The company set out to find a solution that could enable users from any department to access and collaborate on the same customer data. For example, Rosetta Stone wanted to provide its sales personnel with the ability to know if a customer had several service tickets pending so an appropriate strategy regarding how to proceed could be formulated.

THE STRATEGY

In mid-2011, the company considered several options but ultimately decided to adopt Salesforce Service Cloud for the following reasons:

- **Self service.** Service Cloud's knowledge base and self-service portal would enable the company to reduce overall service agent burden by deflecting calls.
- **Increased cross-departmental visibility.** Having already used the Salesforce platform for sales, Rosetta stone was interested in leveraging the ability to provide all of its marketing, sales, and service users with a shared view of customer interactions
- **Scalability.** Rosetta Stone wanted an application that could support extensive growth and integration of new customer data sets as needed.

The process of implementing Service Cloud at Rosetta Stone began in early 2012 with the company contracting consulting firm Astadia to assist with the implementation. Astadia personnel were in charge of development activities and did internal IT configuration for Rosetta Stone. Astadia also did several training sessions with Rosetta Stone personnel in order to help bring them up to speed on how to best navigate the product most efficiently.

Astadia also trained users in five other countries with four different training sessions both locally and via WebEx. Rosetta Stone initially deployed Service Cloud as a separate instance but, shortly after going live, the company integrated it with its other CRM products.

Overall, the Service Cloud deployment took 90 days to complete. The company currently employs one full-time employee to support Service Cloud as well as one developer who devotes 60 to 70 hours a month to Service Cloud. Currently, there are 400 Service Cloud users at Rosetta Stone.

KEY BENEFIT AREAS

As a result of the Service Cloud deployment at Rosetta Stone, the language learning technology provider was able to conduct a higher volume of customer service interactions while redirecting a significant amount of call traffic to its self-service portal and online chat feature.

By adopting Service Cloud, the company was able to shift from a single product to a multiple product business model. If it had done this with Parature, Rosetta Stone would have required more development, administrative effort, and a larger knowledgebase. With Service Cloud, the company was able to sell multiple product versions while segmenting its reps across product lines. Key benefits of the Service Cloud deployment include:

- **Reduced average call handling time.** Before implementing Service Cloud, customer service agents spent an average of 14 minutes on each service phone call. Now that average is closer to nine minutes, resulting in a drop of average call handle time by 20 to 25 percent.
- **Reduced costs from ticket deflections.** Service Cloud ticket deflection allowed service agents to redirect a number of customer tickets to both the self-service portal and to the online chat feature which entails a lower cost to handle than a phone call.
- **Increased product manager productivity.** With Service Cloud, product managers could interact directly with agents via the system and check the status of bug fixes. Service Cloud enabled Rosetta Stone product managers to access this information faster resulting in increased productivity.
- **Improved chat effectiveness.** In addition to driving more people to Service Cloud's online chat feature, Rosetta Stone was able improve the efficacy of chat sessions. It did this by enabling service agents to remote control a customer's application when needed via the integration of such a protocol in the actual Service Cloud solution.
- **Improved visibility into customer data.** As a result of the Service Cloud deployment, Rosetta Stone employees across sales, marketing, and service were able to gain a more holistic view of customers as soon

as data was entered into the application.

As a result of implementing Service Cloud, Rosetta Stone was able to reduce the average service agent call handling time by 20 to 25 percent.

KEY COST AREAS

The largest costs from the Service Cloud deployment were the ongoing software license costs for Service Cloud, consulting costs for Astadia, and the initial cost of management personnel during the 90-day implementation. Other costs from the deployment included training, content translation, travel, and the ongoing personnel to support Service Cloud.

BEST PRACTICES

As companies grow their customer bases, it becomes more and more important to be able to provide the same level of service to customers on multiple channels. Nucleus found that companies moving from legacy applications to Salesforce Service Cloud were able to drive greater agent productivity while reducing the costs associated with such an upgrade (Nucleus Research, p169 — *Guidebook - Upgrading to Salesforce Service Cloud*, October 2015). By enabling users to address customer tickets with chat and e-mail, in addition to the self-service portal, customer service agents are better equipped to handle a larger volume of customer requests while delivering the same level of assistance.

CALCULATING THE ROI

In order to calculate Rosetta Stone's total investment in Salesforce Service Cloud, Nucleus quantified the initial and ongoing costs, over a 3-year period, of software license subscription fees as well as the time it took personnel and consulting firm Astadia to implement and support the application. Employee training time and travel costs were also quantified for training, both domestic and international.

Direct benefits quantified include the eliminated costs of Parature licenses and 1.5 FTEs needed for support after moving to Service Cloud. Indirect benefits quantified include reduced call handling time and increased number of calls deflected.

Not quantified were the increased profits driven from improved customer service.

Salesforce: Building the ROI Business Case

Financial Analysis

Annual ROI: 26% • Payback Period: 3+ years

Benefits	Pre-Start	Year 1	Year 2	Year 3
Direct	0	477,500	605,000	605,000
Indirect	0	386,717	386,717	386,717
Total per period	**0**	**864,217**	**991,717**	**991,717**

Costs—Capitalized Assets	Pre-Start	Year 1	Year 2	Year 3
Software	0	0	0	0
Hardware	0	0	0	0
Project consulting & personnel	0	0	0	0
Total per period	**0**	**0**	**0**	**0**

Costs—Depreciation	Pre-Start	Year 1	Year 2	Year 3
Software	0	0	0	0
Hardware	0	0	0	0
Project consulting & personnel	0	0	0	0
Total per period	**0**	**0**	**0**	**0**

Costs—Depreciation	Pre-Start	Year 1	Year 2	Year 3
Software	750,000	750,000	750,000	0
Hardware	0	0	0	0
Consulting	300,000	0	0	0
Personnel	140,000	116,875	116,875	116,875
Training	66,000	0	0	0
Other	45,000	0	0	0
Total per period	**1,301,000**	**866,875**	**866,875**	**116,875**

Financial Analysis	Results	Year 1	Year 2	Year 3
All government taxes	45%			
Cost of capital	7.0%			
Net cash flow before taxes	(1,301,000)	(2,658)	124,842	874,842
Net cash flow after taxes	(715,550)	(1,462)	68,663	481,163
Annual ROI: direct & indirect benefits				**26%**
Annual ROI: direct benefits only				-4%
Net Present Value (NPV)				(264,171)
Payback period				**3+ years**
Average Annual Cost of Ownership				1,050,542
3-Year IRR				-9%

All calculations are based on Nucleus Research's independent analysis of the expected costs and benefits associated with the solution.

SALESFORCE MARKETING CLOUD
LIFE TIME FITNESS

THE BOTTOM LINE

Life Time Fitness deployed Salesforce Marketing Cloud to modernize its outgoing e-mail marketing. The goal was to connect with each prospect or member in a 1-to-1 relationship. Nucleus found the project enabled Life Time Fitness to better reach prospects and clients, increasing marketing staff productivity while improving member acquisition and engagement.

- ROI: 154%
- Payback: 9 months
- Average annual benefit: $608,297

THE COMPANY

Life Time Fitness is a privately held comprehensive health and lifestyle company that offers a personalized and scientific approach to long-term health and wellness. Services are delivered at resort-like destinations, athletic events, and corporate health events. The program is designed is to help members achieve their personal fitness goals with the support of a team of dedicated professionals and an array of proprietary health assessments. Headquartered in Chanhassen, Minnesota, Life Time opened its first center was opened in 1992. The company operates 119 centers in 26 states and 35 major markets under the Life Time Fitness and Life Time Athletic brands in the United

States and Canada, respectively.

THE CHALLENGE

Life Time and other high-end fitness center operators are facing increasing competition from lower-cost gyms and studio-based exercise programs, such as CrossFit and SoulCycle. The Life Time Fitness mission is to be able to personalize communications with each client for a 1-to-1 relationship. In 2012, Life Time Fitness found that its existing marketing technologies were limiting its ability to effectively compete.

The NCR application the company used was not customizable and could not support targeted marketing because of its inflexibility. Program updates and changes required a long lead time and the expense of additional consulting. Life Time Fitness determined it needed an application that provided flexibility, targeted marketing, and customization to meet its needs and build client cross-channel experiences.

THE STRATEGY

The management team from Life Time Fitness made the decision in January, 2013 to find a new e-mail marketing platform. Due diligence began in March, 2013, and several programs were considered including Yesmail, Oracle Responsys, Experian CheetahMail, and ExactTarget (now Salesforce). After much consideration the company selected Salesforce in June, 2013, for a number of reasons including:

- Life Time determined that Salesforce Marketing Cloud had the most flexible customization services.
- Life Time believed Marketing Cloud was an intuitive platform and easy to use.
- Marketing Cloud could support Life Time's goals of targeted 1-to-1 communications and enable Life Time to build cross-channel marketing programs for each of its clients.

Deployment was initiated in June, 2013, and completed three months later. During those three months, 13 core personnel worked on the migration for 40 percent of their time, while 10 to 15 non-core personnel spent 5 percent of their time on the project.

Back-end systems had to be mapped and integrated to ensure that data could be migrated with accuracy and integrity. This included recreating API integrations to trigger personalized campaigns and analyze feedback from e-mail tracking.

Today Life Time sends more than 7 million e-mails per month. Since its deployment of Marketing Cloud, the company has experienced an 80 percent increase in e-mail open rates.

KEY BENEFIT AREAS

Moving to Marketing Cloud enabled Life Time Fitness to meet its mission of connecting with each of its members through a unique 1-to-1 relationship that will help members achieve their personalized fitness and wellness goals. Marketing Cloud gave Life Time Fitness the ability to segment customer data and create targeted e-mails that enhance both the initial sales process and ongoing client retention. Key benefits of the project included:

- **Increased profits.** Life Time Fitness increased the number of lead-generating e-mails per month, and improved the open rate by 40 percent. Customized mailings increased the number of new memberships, and increased the percentage of conversion to full paying membership.
- **Greater efficiency.** Marketing Cloud improved technology management and eliminated the need for additional personnel to support the NCR platform.
- **Improved marketing productivity.** All e-mails are now dynamic with some form of personalization. Life Time can now meet its monthly goal of 7 to 9 million e-mails and 40 to 50 ad-hoc campaigns annually. Additionally, it can produce cross-channel marketing that was not available with NCR and would have taken additional data scientists to produce.
- **Enhanced customer engagement.** Marketing Cloud improved the member experience with contacts before, during, and after their time at a Life Time Fitness facility, enabling Life Time Fitness to produce targeted follow-up e-mails and identify and address issues as they arise. The increased volume of effective e-mails reduced unsubscribes by 15 percent, and created additional cross-channel sales from existing members.

The growing e-mail marketing platform, soon to include mobile push and SMS messaging, and the unique, personalized member e-mails, have increased member subscriptions to additional Life Time Fitness programs. Additionally, segmentation of e-mail to potential new members is far more effective in attracting new business.

KEY COST AREAS

Costs of the project included software license subscription fees, personnel time to implement and support the application, employee training time, and consulting costs.

BEST PRACTICES

Life Time benefited from Marketing Cloud not only by introducing a new e-mail platform, but by leveraging the cloud benefits of flexibility, scalability, and innovation to drive both initial and ongoing benefit. As Salesforce makes new investments in Marketing Cloud features, the company will be able to take advantage of them with relatively little cost and disruption.

Additionally, the embedding of data science and segmenting capabilities within Marketing Cloud enables the company to produce more segmented and targeted e-mails automatically, a practice that would have required significant investment in internal data science expertise and staff time without the application.

CALCULATING THE ROI

Nucleus quantified the initial and ongoing costs of software license subscription fees, personnel time to implement and support the application, employee training time, and project consulting to calculate Life Time Fitness's total investment in Marketing Cloud.

Direct benefits quantified include cost savings achieved through the elimination of the NCR contract, reduction of current staff, and avoidance of additional hires that would have been needed without Marketing Cloud. Indirect benefits quantified include profits from increased new memberships and increased sales to existing members, which were calculated based on the change in e-mail open rates and related sales conversions, estimated average value, and estimated profit margin.

Financial Analysis

Annual ROI: 154% • Payback Period: 0.7 years

Benefits	Pre-Start	Year 1	Year 2	Year 3
Direct	0	450,150	450,150	450,150
Indirect	0	682,770	682,770	682,770
Total per period	**0**	**1,132,920**	**1,132,920**	**1,132,920**

Costs—Capitalized Assets	Pre-Start	Year 1	Year 2	Year 3
Software	0	0	0	0
Hardware	0	0	0	0
Project consulting & personnel	0	0	0	0
Total per period	**0**	**0**	**0**	**0**

Costs—Depreciation	Pre-Start	Year 1	Year 2	Year 3
Software	0	0	0	0
Hardware	0	0	0	0
Project consulting & personnel	0	0	0	0
Total per period	**0**	**0**	**0**	**0**

Costs—Depreciation	Pre-Start	Year 1	Year 2	Year 3
Software	259,500	332,800	505,217	0
Hardware	0	0	0	0
Consulting	86,000	32,296	2,750	2,750
Personnel	156,600	64,800	64,800	64,800
Training	1,558	0	0	0
Other	0	0	0	0
Total per period	**503,658**	**429,896**	**572,767**	**67,550**

Financial Analysis	Results	Year 1	Year 2	Year 3
All government taxes	45%			
Cost of capital	7.0%			
Net cash flow before taxes	(503,658)	703,024	560,153	1,065,370
Net cash flow after taxes	(277,012)	386,663	308,084	585,954
Annual ROI: direct & indirect benefits				**154%**
Annual ROI:direct benefits only				19%
Net Present Value (NPV)				831,761
Payback period				**0.7 years**
Average Annual Cost of Ownership				524,623
3-Year IRR				129%

All calculations are based on Nucleus Research's independent analysis of the expected costs and benefits associated with the solution.

SALESFORCE COMMUNITY CLOUD
STANLEY HEALTHCARE

THE BOTTOM LINE

Stanley Healthcare deployed Salesforce Community Cloud and Service Cloud to provide customers with self-service support. Nucleus found that the project enabled Stanley to accelerate the resolution of customer and partner issues and inquiries while driving greater staff productivity.

- ROI: 270%
- Payback: 5 months
- Average annual benefit: $929,758

THE COMPANY

Stanley Healthcare provides more than 17,000 healthcare organizations with solutions and analytics to advance the quality of care. Stanley Healthcare products provide safety, security, and process efficiency to benefit healthcare providers with improved efficiency and organizational management. The company is a division of Stanley Black & Decker, a Fortune 500 company.

THE CHALLENGE

Although Stanley had deployed a self-service portal for customers, it was not connected to the company's departments such as sales and operations and did not have community or collaborative capabilities. As the company grew, it recognized that providing a rich self-service environment for customers that could also be leveraged by internal staff and partners could be an important differentiator for its business.

THE STRATEGY

Stanley was already a Salesforce customer and determined that the best product to meet its corporate strategy was to deploy Community Cloud integrated with Service Console for a number of reasons including:

- **Communication.** Stanley Healthcare believed that the interactive cloud-based community would enable customers to shop, return items, apply for licenses, and find key solutions within the collaborative community as quickly and effortlessly as possible.
- **Time to value.** Stanley Healthcare identified that the Community Cloud was an "out of the box" solution requiring minimal customization and had a proven track record for collaborative community interactions, and integrated with the existing Service and Sales Clouds at a reasonable cost.
- **Functionality.** Stanley Healthcare believed that the Service Cloud solution had the flexibility and functionality to support the volume of contacts, avoid the problems of human error inherent to manual processing, and improve data quality.

Stanley Healthcare used Balink to facilitate deployment with custom modifications and technical support. The deployment plan included one week for design, one week for a mock-up and three months for development and testing. Minimal training was required because of the intuitive nature of the application.

KEY BENEFIT AREAS

Community Cloud replaced an inflexible customer portal that was not interactive with the customer, and did not have self-service capabilities. The new application gives the customer multiple options to meet their needs and allows the Stanley Healthcare agent to focus on sales and technical solutions. Key benefits of the Stanley project include:

- **Faster case resolution.** Customer cases requiring agent intervention (with an average volume of 5,000 calls per month) are resolved 15 minutes faster with the new cloud based platform.
- **Increased ticket deflection.** The intuitive and collaborative nature of Community Cloud self service has resulted in significant ticket deflection. This saves, on average, eight minutes per call deflection while providing valuable product insights and knowledge-based problem resolution.
- **Increased revenues.** In addition to time saved and increased agent productivity, each interactive customer contact has become an opportunity to sell additional products and services.
- **Increased customer satisfaction.** Agents' ability to see comprehensive customer information and provide more specific resolutions at the first contact has increased customer satisfaction.

KEY COST AREAS

Costs of the project included software license subscription fees, personnel time to learn, implement, and support the application, and consulting fees.

BEST PRACTICES

Stanley Healthcare found it beneficial to plan the implementation with the use of a professional consultant from the very beginning. This allowed the company to plan the best course of action that would leverage Salesforce for full benefit. For example, comprehensive customer information delivered in the integrated console allows agents to best take advantage of the real-time information and deliver the most appropriate solution. Additionally, the collaborative nature of the Community enables customers to find their own solutions, freeing the Stanley Healthcare agents to focus on resolving complex issues and increase revenue with new sales.

CALCULATING THE ROI

Nucleus quantified the initial and ongoing costs of software license subscription fees, personnel time to implement and support the application, employee training time, and project consulting to calculate the total investment in Stanley's Community Cloud and Service Cloud Console project.

Indirect benefits quantified included the increase in agent productivity, both by ticket deflections through the customer self-service portal, and more rapid access to customer and other information through the integrated service console. These benefits were quantified based on the time saved per case and the average annual fully loaded cost of a customer service agent, using a productivity correction factor to account for the inefficient transfer of time between time saved and additional time worked.

Also quantified as an indirect benefit was the increase in revenues derived from increased customer and company visibility into the warranty and returns process. Not quantified was the increase in customer satisfaction and repeat business driven by a rich and interactive self-service community.

Financial Analysis

Annual ROI: 270% • Payback Period: 0.4 years

Benefits	Pre-Start	Year 1	Year 2	Year 3
Direct	0	0	0	0
Indirect	0	929,758	929,758	929,758
Total per period	**0**	**929,758**	**929,758**	**929,758**

Costs—Capitalized Assets	Pre-Start	Year 1	Year 2	Year 3
Software	0	0	0	0
Hardware	0	0	0	0
Project consulting & personnel	0	0	0	0
Total per period	**0**	**0**	**0**	**0**

Costs—Depreciation	Pre-Start	Year 1	Year 2	Year 3
Software	0	0	0	0
Hardware	0	0	0	0
Project consulting & personnel	0	0	0	0
Total per period	**0**	**0**	**0**	**0**

Costs—Depreciation	Pre-Start	Year 1	Year 2	Year 3
Software	67,200	67,200	67,200	0
Hardware	0	0	0	0
Consulting	170,000	0	0	0
Personnel	82,298	20,250	20,250	20,250
Training	389	0	0	0
Other	0	0	0	0
Total per period	**319,888**	**87,450**	**87,450**	**20,250**

Financial Analysis	Results	Year 1	Year 2	Year 3
All government taxes	45%			
Cost of capital	7.0%			
Net cash flow before taxes	(319,888)	842,308	842,308	909,508
Net cash flow after taxes	(175,938)	463,269	463,269	500,229
Annual ROI: direct & indirect benefits				**270%**
Annual ROI: direct benefits only				-20%
Net Present Value (NPV)				1,069,997
Payback period				**0.4 years**
Average Annual Cost of Ownership				171,679
3-Year IRR				259%

All calculations are based on Nucleus Research's independent analysis of the expected costs and benefits associated with the solution.

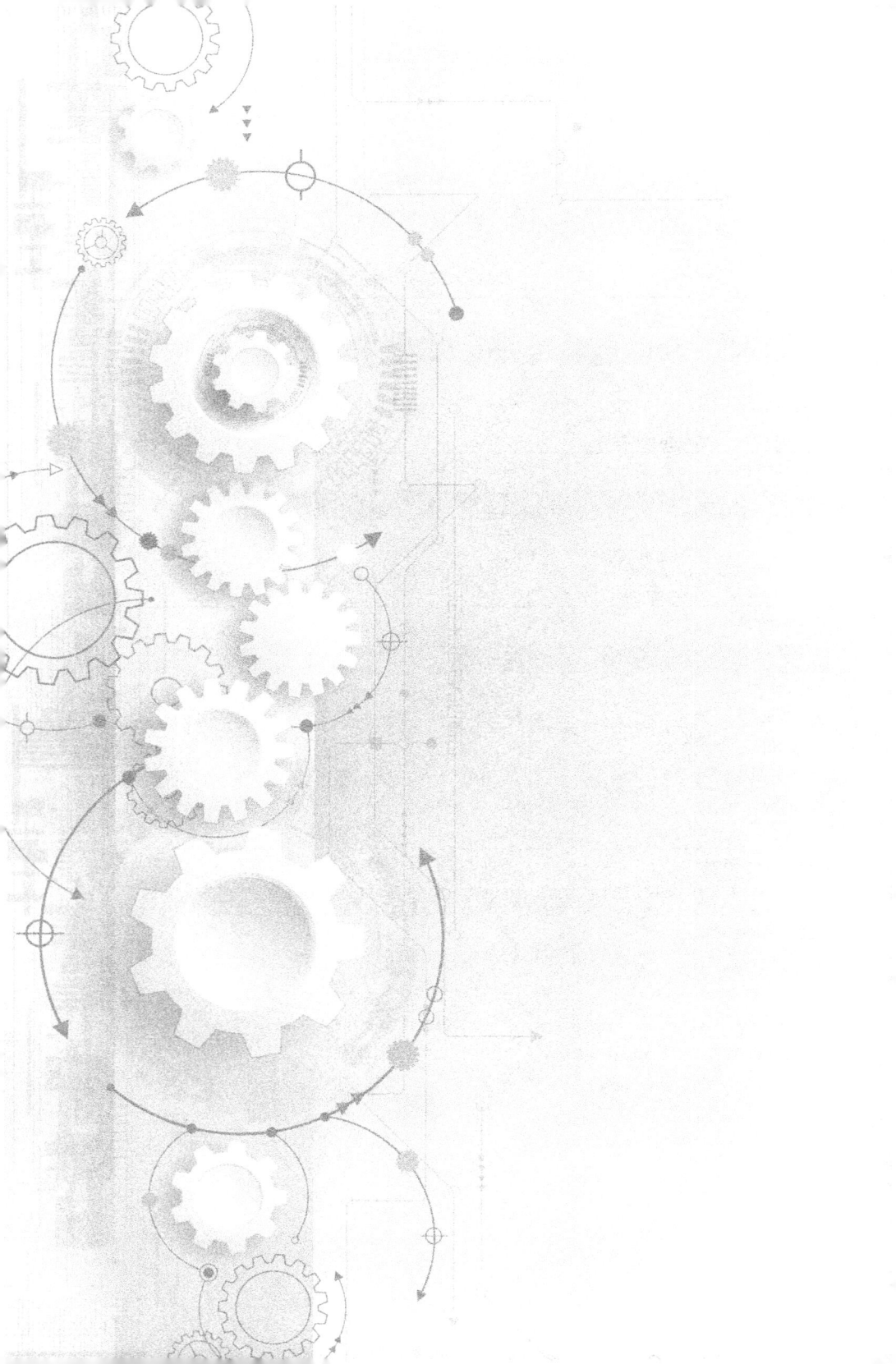

SALESFORCE MARKETING CLOUD
AMPLIFY

THE BOTTOM LINE

Amplify deployed Salesforce Marketing Cloud to replace a decentralized system with a cloud-based marketing solution that would drive future growth. Nucleus found that the project enabled the company to increase the productivity and effectiveness of marketing, optimize advertising spend, and increase revenue.

- ROI: 1079%
- Payback: 16 weeks
- Average annual benefit: $2,784,792

THE COMPANY

Amplify Credit Union is a member-owned financial cooperative with 57,000 members, and eight locations throughout Texas. Amplify's services include personal banking and savings, auto, personal, and real estate loans, wealth management, and commercial banking and lending. Founded in 1967 as IBM Texas Employees Federal Credit Union, Amplify has stayed true to its mission to serve the best interests of its members, providing them with the opportunity to accumulate savings, and to reinvest those savings into its borrowers and communities.

THE CHALLENGE

Prior to Salesforce Marketing Cloud, Amplify relied on a decentralized collection of solutions that made running effective marketing campaigns a challenge. With data stored across 80 systems, retrieving and manipulating it could take multiple hours, and tracking and reporting capabilities were limited. The company recognized the need for one common marketing solution that could maximize the productivity of marketers and help them to execute a more effective marketing strategy.

THE STRATEGY

When the company began exploring marketing solutions, it first considered another marketing solution. After nearly one year of working with the vendor, they reached a roadblock. In September 2015, Amplify was introduced to Salesforce and began exploring its Marketing Cloud solution, along with Sales Cloud, Social Studio, Advertising Studio, and mobile applications. After four months, the decision was made to implement Salesforce Marketing Cloud. Salesforce was selected for the following reasons:

- **Trust and Security.** After running into complications regarding what would happen to member data if the relationship were to end with the other vendor Amplify had considered, Amplify was looking for a vendor which could ensure that its data would remain secure and private. Salesforce's Trust and Security, built natively in the platform, allowed Amplify to take advantage of cloud-based applications without security concerns.
- **Salesforce Ecosystem.** Amplify saw in Salesforce's platform a solution to its bottlenecks in marketing, sales, CRM, advertising, and mobile functionality. What set Salesforce apart from other vendors was its usability, flexibility, cost, and integration capabilities. These features, in tandem with its partners—including Competitor Inbox Insight and Premium Inbox Tools—were attractive to Amplify.

January 31, 2016 Amplify signed with Salesforce to launch the Marketing Cloud and Sales Cloud simultaneously. April 1, 2016 Amplify launched the two solutions, with the assistance of two implementation partners—Shell Black and Perry Software—who also assisted with on-the-job training.

KEY BENEFIT AREAS

By implementing Salesforce Marketing Cloud, Amplify increased the effectiveness and productivity of its marketing team, optimized campaigns, and increased its revenue. Nucleus assessed the direct and indirect benefits associated with Amplify's implementation of Salesforce Marketing Cloud, and found that benefits included:

- **Increased marketing productivity.** With Salesforce Marketing Cloud, marketers increased their efficiency. For example, time devoted to running reports decreased by 98 percent, from 120 hours to three hours per month. Without Salesforce Marketing Cloud, Amplify estimates it would need four additional full-time marketing employees to do the same amount of work its marketing department does now, leading to annual savings of over $300,000 in employee salary alone *Reporting time decreased by 98 percent, and over $300,000 in employee salary alone was saved annually.*
- **Improved effectiveness of marketing.** Salesforce Marketing Cloud significantly improved the effectiveness of the marketing department by improving lead generation and client engagement.
  - Amplify increased the number of leads generated for the same advertising spend by 50 percent, using its own CRM data to target advertising.
  - Using look-alike audience functionality and Journey Builder, Amplify increased e-mail open rates by 45 percent and click-through rates by 20 percent.
- **Optimized campaigns.** Amplify estimates it would have needed to double its advertising spend with its prior marketing program to achieve the same number of leads per month as it does now. Salesforce Marketing Cloud, therefore, decreased Amplify's cost per lead by 50 percent. *Amplify increased leads by 50 percent, e-mail open rates by 45 percent, and click-through rates by 20 percent, while decreasing the cost per lead by 50 percent.*
- **Increased revenue.** Salesforce Marketing Cloud has directly impacted revenue. Implementing the solution led to an annual net profit of over $1.4 million, and a 400 percent increase in revenue for Amplify's outbound sales team. *Implementing Salesforce Marketing Cloud led to an annual net profit of over $1.4 million, and a 400 percent increase in*

revenue for Amplify's outbound sales team.

KEY COST AREAS

The greatest cost of the project was personnel costs—initial and ongoing—which amounted to 60 percent of the total costs. Other costs included software and consulting costs.

BEST PRACTICES

Prior to Salesforce, Amplify spent over one year considering another vendor that did not end up suiting the needs of the business. To avoid delaying deployment, companies should consider several vendors and select the one that best suits their needs, taking all factors—such as functionality, usability, and compliance—into account. Had Amplify considered Salesforce initially alongside the other vendor, it would have one additional year of experiencing the benefits of Salesforce Marketing Cloud.

CALCULATING THE ROI

To calculate the total investment made in Salesforce Marketing Cloud, Nucleus quantified, over a three-year period, the initial and ongoing costs of personnel, software subscriptions, and consulting. Direct benefits quantified included increased revenue, optimized advertising spend, and hiring savings, which was calculated based on the average annual fully loaded cost of an employee using a productivity correction factor to account for the inefficient transfer of time between time saved and additional time worked. Indirect benefits quantified included increased marketing productivity through increased reporting speed, and improved effectiveness of marketing through improved lead generation and engagement.

The cumulative net benefit represented in the graphic is presented in US dollars and is calculated by aggregating the net benefit over the three years of the study. The net cash flows represented in the graphic is also presented in US dollars and represents the cash inflows and outflows associated with the project from initial investment through the 3-year period analyzed.

Salesforce Marketing Cloud: Amplify

Financial Analysis

Annual ROI: 1079% • Payback Period: 0.3 years

Benefits	Pre-Start	Year 1	Year 2	Year 3
Direct	0	1,189,250	2,811,500	4,353,625
Indirect	0	0	0	0
Total per period	**0**	**1,189,250**	**2,811,500**	**4,353,625**

Costs—Capitalized Assets	Pre-Start	Year 1	Year 2	Year 3
Software	0	0	0	0
Hardware	0	0	0	0
Project consulting & personnel	0	0	0	0
Total per period	**0**	**0**	**0**	**0**

Costs—Depreciation	Pre-Start	Year 1	Year 2	Year 3
Software	0	0	0	0
Hardware	0	0	0	0
Project consulting & personnel	0	0	0	0
Total per period	**0**	**0**	**0**	**0**

Costs—Depreciation	Pre-Start	Year 1	Year 2	Year 3
Software	115,438	115,438	115,438	0
Hardware	0	0	0	0
Consulting	8,000	54,192	54,192	6,192
Personnel	105,402	215,663	192,038	192,038
Training	0	0	0	0
Other	0	0	0	0
Total per period	**228,840**	**385,293**	**361,668**	**198,230**

Financial Analysis	Results	Year 1	Year 2	Year 3
All government taxes	45%			
Cost of capital	7.0%			
Net cash flow before taxes	(228,840)	803,958	2,449,833	4,155,396
Net cash flow after taxes	(125,862)	442,177	1,347,408	2,285,468
Annual ROI: direct & indirect benefits				**1079%**
Annual ROI: direct benefits only				1079%
Net Present Value (NPV)				3,329,888
Payback period				**0.3 years**
Average Annual Cost of Ownership				391,343
3-Year IRR				487%

All calculations are based on Nucleus Research's independent analysis of the expected costs and benefits associated with the solution.

SALESFORCE ESSENTIALS
5P CONSULTING

THE BOTTOM LINE

5P Consulting deployed Salesforce Essentials to create a single, unified repository for customer and account data. It utilizes automation and artificial intelligence (AI) to surface relevant insights and eliminate manual processes like data entry, and to increase lead generation with a Web-to-lead integration. By implementing Salesforce Essentials, 5P Consulting tripled lead generation, saved each user approximately four hours per week from eliminated data entry and time spent searching for records, and avoided a business development hire. The software was implemented and ready to use within a week, and delivers an ROI of 998 percent to 5P Consulting.

- ROI: 998%
- Payback: 1.2 months

THE COMPANY

5P Consulting is a boutique consulting company that specializes in management and solutions consulting for its diverse set of clients. As a technology consultant, it is not like traditional small businesses that are reluctant to invest in new technology, as it sees firsthand how strategic technology projects can transform businesses. It helps customers optimize the people, processes, and technology that run businesses. Examples of the services 5P provides include growth planning, streamlining processes and implement automation (where applicable) to operate more efficiently, data management and analytics strategy, developing and executing information technology (IT) strategy, and traditional executive training and management consulting.

THE CHALLENGE

As a boutique consulting group, 5P was aware of the benefits and improvements that implementing an effective and integrated customer relationship management (CRM) system can deliver. It had identified that Salesforce met its needs; however, with a user group of only five leadership team members, buying professional or enterprise edition Salesforce licenses was unfeasible. When Salesforce Essentials—the CRM that caters specifically to small businesses—became available, 5P was able to affordably implement Salesforce.

As consultants whose business is built around helping clients optimize their organizations by strategy, process, and systems, the company is experienced in successful software implementations. It identified the following capabilities and features that the system needed to deliver in order to add value:

- **Centralize data** to ensure all users have a unified view of the company and minimize time spent searching for data and duplication of effort from manually entering data.
- **Support the lead-to-cash cycle.** Web-to-lead integrations automatically populate Website traffic into the CRM system as leads. Additionally, the system should have the ability to track cases automatically throughout the sales pipe and surface relevant account updates to guide outreach.
- **Create shared dashboards and reports** to track key performance indicators and provide a single source of truth for the leadership team to track company health and progress toward goals.

THE STRATEGY

The core functionality was implemented in approximately twelve hours. The CEO spent two hours customizing some aspects of the interface, implementing the email inbox integration with Salesforce, and adding other users to the system. The CEO was also responsible for establishing organization-wide communication to drive adoption. A principal architect spent approximately ten hours on customer contact and account data migration, configuring the Web-to-lead system, and creating the reusable reports and dashboards. Some additional hours were needed to complete an integration with Docusign for electronic document signage and sharing, however the core CRM functionality was up and running after the twelve hours of implementation work.

The system is easy to maintain and requires virtually no regular ongoing support. There are currently five users on the system. It is used by company leadership to unify and formalize the lead-to-cash system, giving the entire team visibility to account activity and the ability to coordinate customer more efficiently outreach without duplicating effort. The next step for 5P is to implement the customer service component of Essentials. The vision is that when customers call in with requests or questions, the system would automatically create a ticket and log it within Salesforce, allowing for better tracking and visibility to service cases.

KEY BENEFIT AREAS

Key benefit areas seen as a result of the Salesforce Essentials deployment include cost savings from an avoided business development hire, increased user productivity by reducing duplication of data entry and time spent searching for customer information, increased lead generation from Web-to-lead configuration, and increased data transparency and visibility for company leadership to assess more accurately the health of the company.

- **Avoided business development hire.** With the uniform visibility to account information, the leadership team was able to formalize a business development process. Now each member of the team is responsible for bringing in two new leads per week and converting two of those leads to opportunities per month. This is a more standardized and process-driven approach to business development than was possible before Salesforce; it allowed the company to avoid hiring one full-time equivalent business development staffer.
- **Increased user productivity.** Centralizing all operations and data on the Salesforce system reduced the duplication of efforts in data entry and cut down on time spent searching for account information. These efficiency improvements allowed each of the five users to save four hours per week on average.
- **Increased lead generation.** Since implementing Salesforce Essentials,

5P has tripled its lead generation rate. It implemented Web-to-lead functionality which automatically creates leads from inbound traffic to the company websites. Additionally, the integration with Gmail allows inbound email traffic to be automatically populated in the system.
- **Increased data transparency and visibility to sales pipeline.** The shared dashboards and reports appear on the Salesforce homepage upon logging in, so all users have access to the same up-to-date data regarding sales pipeline and company health. This has allowed the company to reduce meetings spent coordinating the sales pipeline and has increased trust in data company wide.

KEY COST AREAS

The largest cost area of the 5P Consulting deployment was the cost of approximately twelve hours of personnel time for the implementation of the Salesforce software. The other cost over the three-year period was the Salesforce Essentials licenses.

BEST PRACTICES

Two of the most valuable aspects of the Salesforce instance to 5P are the dashboards and reports that are automatically displayed to all users from the home screen upon logging in. This ensures that the users always have a single source of truth that accurately displays sales and company performance metrics. This streamlines leadership meetings because all participants are accustomed to viewing the same data and can proactively address issues as they arise. Configuring the Salesforce Inbox plugin was key for the organization as well because it eliminates data entry for email activity. In addition to populating the Salesforce system with data from emails automatically, the plugin helps train Salesforce Einstein— Salesforce's artificial intelligence technology—which in turn helps surface relevant updates and recommendations for each account to aid in converting leads to sales.

On a high level, this shows how 5P was able to take advantage of the technology available to them to automate repeated processes and benefit from advances in AI technology with Einstein.

CALCULATING THE ROI

Nucleus Research analyzed the costs of software, hardware, personnel, professional services, and user training over a three-year period to quantify 5P Consulting's total investment in Salesforce technology. Direct and indirect benefits were also quantified over the three-year period.

Direct benefits quantified included the cost savings realized from an avoided business development hire.

Indirect benefits quantified included time savings from reduced data entry, duplication of effort, and time spent searching for account information. We calculated the time savings benefit using the fully loaded cost per hour of employees. Time savings were multiplied by a correction factor to account for the inefficient transfer of time between time saved and additional time worked.

Salesforce: Building the ROI Business Case

Financial Analysis

Annual ROI: 998% • Payback Period: 0.1 years

Benefits	Pre-Start	Year 1	Year 2	Year 3
Direct	0	100,000	100,000	100,000
Indirect	0	20,800	20,800	20,800
Total per period	**0**	**120,800**	**120,800**	**120,800**

Costs—Capitalized Assets	Pre-Start	Year 1	Year 2	Year 3
Software	0	0	0	0
Hardware	0	0	0	0
Project consulting & personnel	0	0	0	0
Total per period	**0**	**0**	**0**	**0**

Costs—Depreciation	Pre-Start	Year 1	Year 2	Year 3
Software	0	0	0	0
Hardware	0	0	0	0
Project consulting & personnel	0	0	0	0
Total per period	**0**	**0**	**0**	**0**

Costs—Depreciation	Pre-Start	Year 1	Year 2	Year 3
Software	1,500	1,500	1,500	0
Hardware	0	0	0	0
Consulting	0	0	0	0
Personnel	10,500	0	0	0
Training	0	0	0	0
Other	0	0	0	0
Total per period	**12,000**	**1,500**	**1,500**	**0**

Financial Analysis	Results	Year 1	Year 2	Year 3
All government taxes	45%			
Cost of capital	7.0%			
Net cash flow before taxes	(12,000)	119,300	119,300	120,800
Net cash flow after taxes	(6,600)	65,615	65,615	66,440
Annual ROI: direct & indirect benefits				**998%**
Annual ROI: direct benefits only				825%
Net Present Value (NPV)				166,268
Payback period				**0.1 years**
Average Annual Cost of Ownership				5,000
3-Year IRR				994%

All calculations are based on Nucleus Research's independent analysis of the expected costs and benefits associated with the solution.

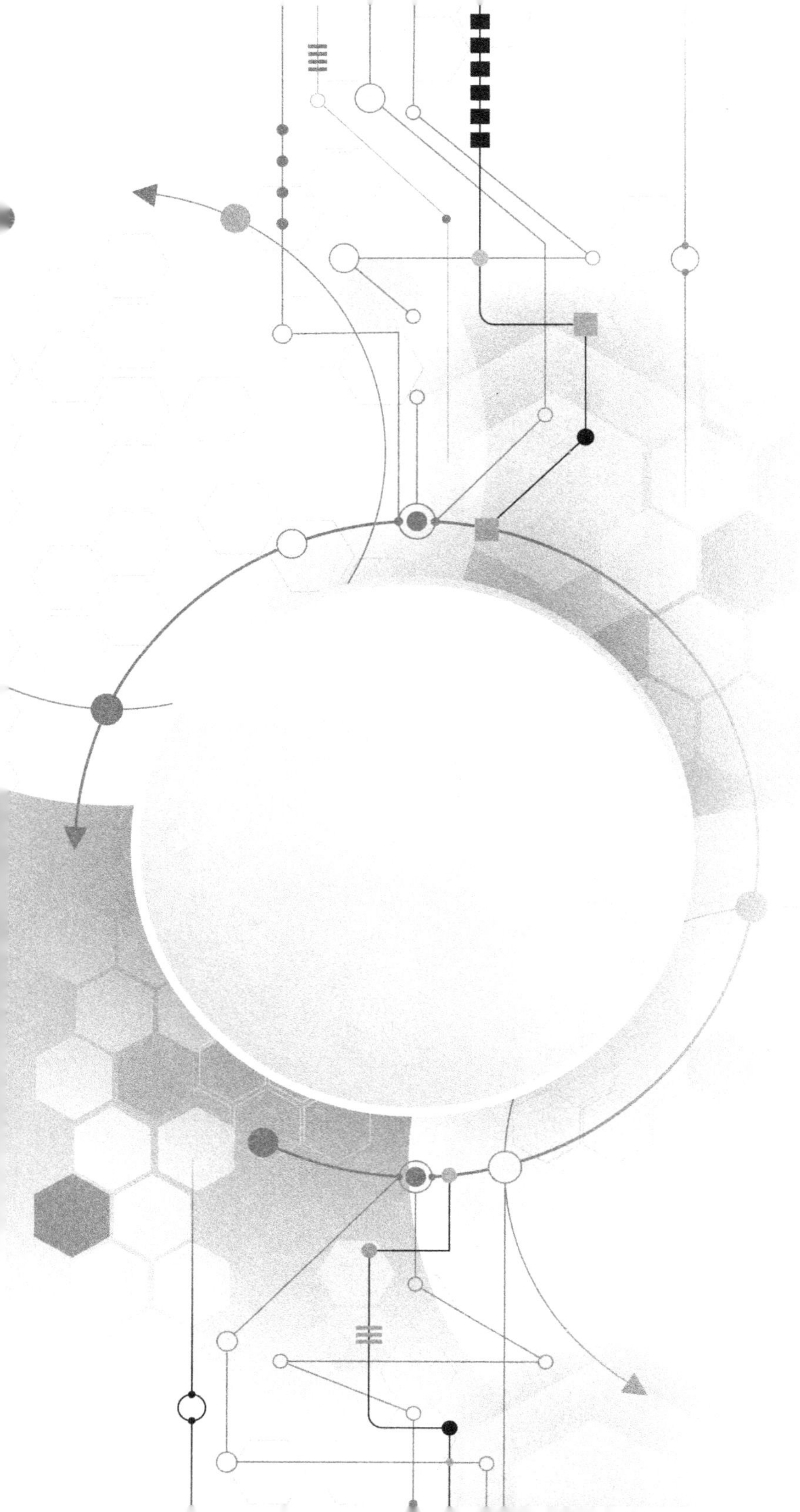

CONCLUSION

The pace of technology development is accelerating. It is a constant trend we've seen since before 1950. The introduction of the PC in the early 80s represented a quantum leap, as did the commercialization of the Internet in the 90s and the emergence of cloud computing in the 2000s.

Making the right tech. decisions only gets more challenging as we go forward—especially now that we are seeing highly divergent solutions, giving us serious options for our businesses.

The result is technology playing an even more central role in most businesses. From automated processes to tighter, better applications, technology has the ability to help a business break out—or fail. And these decisions are not made in a vacuum. Your competitors are also evaluating their options. So, it's not only about nailing the decision on your end, but knowing that a misstep could give a competitor a serious leg up. The biggest shift in thinking about tech. decisions is to focus on what your business challenges and needs are, and not force-fitting your business processes into what several leading vendors can offer.

We see a number of areas that you should consider in making tech. decisions.

Integration

Integration of enterprise software applications will not only continue but accelerate going forward. With the spread of the cloud, it is getting easier to integrate CRM, ERP, HCM, supply chain, data management, analytics, and other applications. At some point, the applications become so integrated that CRM is viewed as a feature set of the mega-app rather than a standalone, alongside the ERP feature set. From a decision-making perspective, look for solutions that have preintegration and even certification to work with other apps used by your organization.

Increase the cadence of your tech. reviews

Career experts say that employees should review new opportunities every six months, whether they are actively looking or not. There is a benefit in knowing what is out there and weighing options, and that applies to executives in charge of making tech. decisions. An annual review these days is irresponsible and even six months is too long, especially with the steady stream of analytics coming in with metrics and insight into performance. We have become a continuous world that is always "on"; that's especially true of technology.

Even if you are reviewing technology often, take time to look at the big picture and consider new options — and do it more often.

I hope this book gives you some clarity into assessing Salesforce and making better decisions. With an eye on business value now and building more value in the future, dig into what's out there, give it a candid and honest look, and make the best decision to grow your business. As the competition grows, technology can either help you play offense and pull ahead of your rivals or put you on the defensive trying to catch up to them.

Good luck!

ABOUT THE AUTHOR

Daniel Elman is the Principal Analyst at Nucleus Research for its customer relationship management (CRM) and analytics programs. Daniel has written extensively about the respective CRM and analytics markets, as well as machine learning and AI, containerization, marketing automation, and transitioning from on-premises to cloud deployment. In 2018 he graduated from Boston University with a BA in Pure and Applied Mathematics where he also researched Lie groups and black hole superradiance. Before moving to Boston, Daniel grew up in Massena, New York.

ABOUT NUCLEUS RESEARCH

Nucleus Research is a global provider of investigative, case-based technology research and advisory services. We deliver the numbers that drive business decisions.

For more information, visit NucleusResearch.com or follow us on Twitter at @NucleusResearch.

NUCLEUS RESEARCH

100 State Street · Boston, MA 02109 · +1 617-720-2000
www.NucleusResearch.com

CPSIA information can be obtained
at www.ICGtesting.com
Printed in the USA
LVHW092358120420
653202LV00002B/361